access to history

USA
and VIETNAM
1945 – 75

Vivienne Sanders

access to history

The USA
and VIETNAM
1945 – 75

Vivienne Sanders

Hodder & Stoughton

A MEMBER OF THE HODDER HEADLINE GROUP

For John Apgar; I hope I got it right

Orders: please contact Bookpoint Ltd, 39 Milton Park, Abingdon, Oxon OX14 4TD. Telephone: (44) 01235 400414, Fax: (44) 01235 400454. Lines are open from 9.00 - 6.00, Monday to Saturday, with a 24 hour message answering service. Email address: orders@bookpoint.co.uk

British Library Cataloguing in Publication Data

A catalogue for this title is available from the British Library

ISBN 0 340 701 935

First published 1998

Impression number	10	9	8	7	6	5	4	3	2	1
Year		2004	2003	2002	2001	2000	1999	1998		

Cover photo from Corbis, photo by Tim Page

Illustrations by Ian Foulis & Associates Ltd, Saltash
Typeset by Sempringham publishing services, Bedford
Printed in Great Britain for Hodder & Stoughton Educational,
a division of Hodder Headline Plc, 338 Euston Road, London NW1 3BH
by Redwood Books, Trowbridge, Wiltshire.

Contents

Preface

To the general reader

Although the *Access to History* series has been designed with the needs of students studying the subject at higher examination levels very much in mind, it also has a great deal to offer the general reader. The main body of the text (i.e. ignoring the 'Study Guides' at the ends of chapters) forms a readable and yet stimulating survey of a coherent topic as studied by historians. However, each author's aim has not merely been to provide a clear explanation of what happened in the past (to interest and inform): it has also been assumed that most readers wish to be stimulated into thinking further about the topic and to form opinions of their own about the significance of the events that are described and discussed (to be challenged). Thus, although no prior knowledge of the topic is expected on the reader's part, she or he is treated as an intelligent and thinking person throughout. The author tends to share ideas and possibilities with the reader, rather than passing on numbers of so-called 'historical truths'.

To the student reader

There are many ways in which the series can be used by students studying history at a higher level. It will, therefore, be worthwhile thinking about your own study strategy before you start your work on this book. Obviously, your strategy will vary depending on the aim you have in mind, and the time for study that is available to you.

If, for example, you want to acquire a general overview of the topic in the shortest possible time, the following approach will probably be the most effective:

1. Read Chapter 1 and think about its contents.
2. Read the 'Making notes' section at the end of Chapter 2 and decide whether it is necessary for you to read this chapter.
3. If it is, read the chapter, stopping at each heading to note down the main points that have been made.
4. Repeat stage 2 (and stage 3 where appropriate) for all the other chapters.

If, however, your aim is to gain a thorough grasp of the topic, taking however much time is necessary to do so, you may benefit from carrying out the same procedure with each chapter, as follows:

1. Read the chapter as fast as you can, and preferably at one sitting.
2. Study the flow diagram at the end of the chapter, ensuring that you understand the general 'shape' of what you have just read.

3. Read the 'Making notes' section (and the 'Answering essay questions' section, if there is one) and decide what further work you need to do on the chapter. In particularly important sections of the book, this will involve reading the chapter a second time and stopping at each heading to think about (and to write a summary of) what you have just read.

4. Attempt the 'Source-based questions' section. It will sometimes be sufficient to think through your answers, but additional understanding will often be gained by forcing yourself to write them down.

When you have finished the main chapters of the book, study the 'Further Reading' section and decide what additional reading (if any) you will do on the topic.

This book has been designed to help make your studies both enjoyable and successful. If you can think of ways in which this could have been done more effectively, please write to tell me. In the meantime, I hope that you will gain greatly from your study of History.

Keith Randell

Acknowledgements

The Publishers would like to thank the following for permission to reproduce material in this volume:

Yale University Press for extracts from *Lodge in Vietnam* by Anne Blair (1995); extracts reprinted by permission of Fourth Estate Ltd from *Giap: The Victor in Vietnam* by Peter Macdonald © 1993 by Peter Macdonald; Hutchinson for extracts from *Vietnam a History* by S Karnow (1991); Routledge for an extract from *The Vietnam Reader* ed. W Capps (1990); Faber and Faber for extracts from *Kennedy v. Khrushchev, The Crisis Years* by Michael Beschloss (1991); University Press of Kansas for extracts from *The Presidency of John F Kennedy* by James N Giglio (1991) and *The Presidency of Lyndon B Johnson* by Vaughn Davis Bornet (1983); McGraw-Hill for the extract from *To Reason Why* ed. JP Kimball (1990).

The Publishers would like to thank the following for permission to reproduce the following copyright illustrations:
The photograph on the front cover was reproduced courtesy of Corbis (photo by Tim Page). Page 29 (left) Michigan State University Archives and Historical Collections,(right) Howard Sochinek Life Magazine © 1995 Time Inc; page 77 Associated Press, London; page 79 Magnum Photos, London; page 98 Associated Press, London.

1 Introduction: America and Vietnam

Many who were born after the American involvement in the Vietnam war ended (1973) have vivid mental images of Americans in Vietnam, thanks to memorable scenes in Hollywood movies. Robin Williams as a DJ trying to win the hearts and minds of the Vietnamese people in *Good Morning Vietnam*; Robert de Niro trying to stop his Vietnam veteran buddy playing Russian roulette with a gun against his head in *The Deer Hunter*; Charlie Sheen prowling through the jungle with a war-crazed sergeant in *Platoon*; Sylvester Stallone going back to Indochina to defeat the Communists single handedly in a *Rambo* film; Tom Cruise barely recognisable as a crippled veteran in *Born on the Fourth of July*.

The Vietnam war is still very much alive in the memories and actions of Americans today. I spent Christmas 1995 with my uncle and aunt in California. A career soldier in his younger days, my uncle was a helicopter pilot in the American army in Vietnam in 1967-8. I wanted to hear his recollections of Vietnam. 'When Bob [his son] comes,' my uncle said, 'don't mention the war. It is not the sort of thing I want to talk about in front of my kids.' I knew the great issues which historians debate about America and Vietnam, but many were painfully immediate that Christmas. My uncle was a professional soldier in the army of the richest and most powerful nation in the world in 1967. Why did he have to fight in a backward country in Southeast Asia? Why does he think his children are embarrassed about his participation in the war? What impact did the war have on him and his family?

1 A Brief Summary of America and Vietnam

From 1946 to 1954 the Vietnamese people struggled for independence against their French colonial masters. When the French left Vietnam in 1954 the country was temporarily divided into two states - South Vietnam and North Vietnam. Almost immediately the Americans moved in, helping to create and support an anti-Communist Vietnamese regime in the south against the Communist Vietnamese regime in the north. Although Vietnamese struggles against foreigners before 1954 are briefly discussed, this book concentrates on the years of American involvement in Vietnam (1954-73). From 1954, America made increasingly strenuous efforts to support the government of South Vietnam in its struggle against subversive indigenous Communist guerrillas who were supported by North Vietnam, China and the USSR. However, by 1973 America had given up the struggle against the Vietnamese Communists. The latter proceeded to take over the whole of Vietnam in 1975. The causes, course and consequences of American involvement are much debated by historians, and each chapter in this book is designed to familiarise you with the main areas of disagreement between historians and to help you make up your own mind about the issues. The story is covered chronologically, and within the chronological framework each president's policy is analysed. The chronological table (page 142) is a useful reminder of the overall pattern of events.

2 Historians' Debates

Historians disagree about almost every aspect of America's involvement in Vietnam. There is not even agreement about the dates between which America was at war. This is because American diplomatic and military intervention was gradual. It escalated slowly, over a long period of time from 1945 onwards. Furthermore, America never actually declared war on anyone. There was little direct involvement between 1945 and 1954 when France was attempting to re-establish colonial rule over the country following the period of Japanese occupation during the Second World War (see Chapters 2 and 3), but from 1954 onwards America became more and more embroiled in the region (Chapters 4 to 8).

One of the most hotly debated issues is why America got involved and remained in Vietnam. The official American government position was that America was fighting against an aggressive and evil Communist movement, and that the Vietnamese Communists were the puppets of the USSR and China. America's government said that if Vietnam fell to Communism, other Southeast Asian countries would probably follow (for this 'domino theory' see page 22). Unless America stopped Communism, American national security and liberty and free enterprise throughout the world would be threatened. There were different emphases as circumstances changed. In the 1950s it was stressed that America's ally France needed help (Chapters 2 and 3). In the 1960s South Vietnam's need for freedom and democracy was emphasised (Chapters 4 to 8). It was said that America had an obligation to continue its commitment in Vietnam and that American international credibility would be damaged if America withdrew (see especially Chapters 5, 7 and 8). While some historians see idealism behind America's anti-Communist crusading, others think that American economic self-interest was the most important motivating force. Many companies did well out of war, and many Americans thought it vital that America should continue to have access to the raw materials and markets of Southeast Asia - something they thought would cease if Southeast Asia became Communist (see page 22). Many Vietnamese today blame American economic greed and militarism.

Historians argue over how the blame for the involvement and its continuation should be apportioned between the various presidents who held office during this period. Truman (1945-53) (Chapter 2) was the first to get involved but he usually gets off lightly; some blame Eisenhower (1953-61) (Chapter 3); more blame Kennedy (1961-3) (Chapter 4); and most blame Johnson (1963-9) (Chapters 5 to 7). Many revile Nixon (1969-73) (Chapter 8) for not getting America out fast enough. Some historians favour the 'quagmire' interpretation of American involvement: successive presidents took one step after another, thinking each step would be the one to solve the Vietnam problem; America then got deeper and deeper into the quagmire (literally, a muddy marsh). Some historians bitterly accuse American presidents of knowing that they could not win yet continuing the war so that they would not be 'the first president to lose a war'. That is known as the 'stalemate' theory. Other historians feel it is unfair to blame the presidents alone. They argue that the presidents' advisers bear some responsibility, as do the national security bureaucracies and institutions, the State Department, the Defence Department, the Joint Chiefs of Staff (JCS), the Central Intelligence Agency (CIA), and ambassadors to Vietnam. Presidents normally make decisions after hearing the advice of all the above. Furthermore, in order to finance any fighting, the president needed to get money from Congress. The president and Congress were elected by the people. Some historians claim that Congress, the public, and the press who kept them informed bear some responsibility for American involvement because it is clear that presidents responded to what they thought the electorate did or did not want.

Which interpretation is right? As you read the rest of the book you will probably conclude that the right answer lies in a combination of all of them. You will decide for yourself how much of the blame should be allocated to each group or individual.

The other central debate concerns why America failed in the war (Chapters 6 to 7). Despite tremendous American efforts, the state of South Vietnam collapsed in 1975 after an invasion by the North. The American military tend to blame the civilians for the loss of the war. Had America immediately employed all its military power, they argue, it would have won. They are bitter about the politicians who 'lost their nerve' in the face of mounting protests from the American public. Others blame the military as much as the civilians, saying they failed to adopt the appropriate counter-insurgency tactics. Instead of 'search and destroy' operations against the Communist guerrillas, America should have concentrated forces on the 17th parallel to divide the North and South (see the map on page 25), and worked harder to win the hearts and minds of the South Vietnamese people. Some believe the war was unwinnable because of the strength and stubborn conviction of the North Vietnamese (helped by the USSR and China) and the hopelessness of America's South Vietnamese allies.

The results of the war are less debated. It is unanimously agreed that Americans and Vietnamese suffered physically, emotionally and economically (Chapters 6 to 8). There are still visible reminders of the war. Limbless veterans and war memorials can be seen in both countries. The physical landscape in Vietnam has not yet recovered. Lush tropical forests have not yet grown back. So many Vietnamese emigrated to America that one area of Los Angeles is known as 'Little Saigon'. Some remain embittered in both countries, although more are keen to forget the war and get on with their lives. Perhaps the final great debate about 'Vietnam' is what, if any, lessons America (and others) can learn from it (Chapter 8).

Studying 'Introduction to America and Vietnam'

Before moving on to read the next chapter, check that you have understood the great debates about America and Vietnam that have been introduced in this chapter. Keep the debates in mind as you read about each president. As you read Chapters 2 to 5 ask yourself why each president got involved in Vietnam. What were his motives? To what extent was he influenced by his predecessors, his military and civilian advisers and by domestic politics? As early as Chapter 2, start seeking reasons for the American failure. In Chapter 6 in particular, ask yourself whether or not that failure was inevitable. When reading Chapters 6, 7 and 8, ask yourself why Johnson and Nixon felt they had to retreat, and assess the wisdom of the way in which they retreated. You will get ideas about the results and impact of the war throughout the book but particularly in Chapters 6, 7 and 8.

Summary Diagram
Introduction: America and Vietnam

Debates

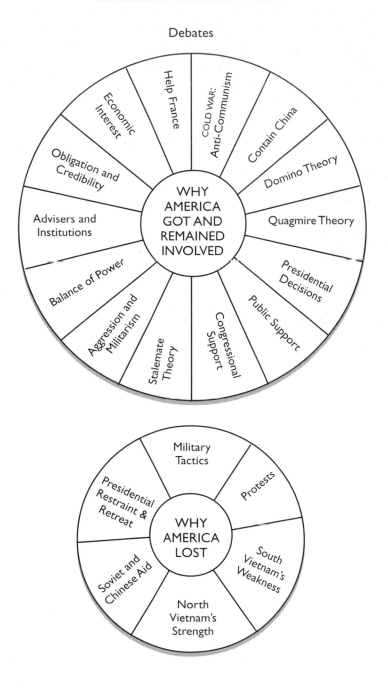

2 Vietnam and Foreigners to 1953

There are three particularly controversial questions regarding American involvement in Vietnam. Why did America get involved? Which presidents were responsible for that involvement? Why did America fail there? This chapter will give some answers to these three questions, within a chronological framework. The chapter introduces the Vietnamese nationalist tradition, helping to explain why the Chinese and then the French could not sustain domination of Vietnam. The Chinese and French failures are important to remember when trying to understand America's subsequent problems in Vietnam. The chapter then explains why Presidents Roosevelt (1933-45) and Truman (1945-53) were interested in Vietnam, and how Truman got involved in helping the unpopular French colonialists there.

1 Ho Chi Minh and Vietnamese Nationalism

Two of the most important reasons why the Americans were to fail in Vietnam were Vietnamese nationalism and the leadership of Ho Chi Minh (1890-1969). In order to understand Vietnamese nationalism and Ho, their history before American intervention has to be investigated.

a) Threats to Vietnamese Independence Before 1900

Captain John White was the first American to set foot on Vietnamese soil. Seeking trade, he arrived in the port of Saigon in 1820. He found a small country very different from the United States of America. The vast majority of Vietnamese were peasant farmers producing rice on the fertile deltas of the Red River in the north and the Mekong in the south. The growing of rice was a communal activity carried out by the people of each village. Their community spirit and nationalism had been vital in fending off frequent Chinese attempts to conquer Vietnam. China was at least a hundred times larger in both area and population, but during their centuries of struggle against the Chinese the Vietnamese had generally been successful because they had perfected guerrilla warfare techniques. Vietnamese guerrillas abandoned the towns, avoided frontal attacks, and harassed the Chinese into confusion and exhaustion.

During the nineteenth century the French replaced the Chinese as the greatest threat to Vietnamese independence. In their search for souls, trade, empire and glory, the French began attacking Vietnam in the mid-nineteenth century. By 1887 the countries subsequently known as Vietnam, Cambodia and Laos were under the control of the French who referred to them collectively as Indochina. Vietnamese internal squabbles had facilitated the French triumph, but the economic and political humiliations of French colonial rule soon caused articulate Vietnamese nationalists to unite to consider how to turn national resentment into rebellion. One nationalist who changed his name many times (partly to avoid detection) eventually became known throughout the world as Ho Chi Minh.

b) The Making of a Revolutionary Nationalist

Ho Chi Minh's father worked his way up to the rank of mandarin (a top civil servant), then abandoned his family and became a travelling teacher and doctor. Ho inherited that urge to serve and wander, free of family commitments. In 1911 he sailed away from Vietnam on a French merchant ship and it was 30 years before he returned. On his travels he studied westerners with interest and admiration. He was particularly impressed by the wealth and dynamism of New York City, where thrusting skyscrapers left him awe-struck. He took any job, whether assistant pastry cook in London's five-star Carlton Hotel or painter of 'genuine' Chinese antiquities in France! Intoxicated by French culture during a six-year-stay in Paris, he denounced the corruption of the French language by English words such as 'le manager'. He mixed with political radicals who discussed socialism and the Communist revolution currently convulsing Russia. Ho discovered that he shared many Communist beliefs, especially opposition to the colonialism whereby white nations dominated Asians and Africans. In 1919 America's President Woodrow Wilson was in France masterminding the peace settlement at the end of the First World War. Wilson emphasised that all people had the right to self-determination (the right to decide how they would be governed). Ho was impressed by Wilson's ideas and the words of the American Declaration of Independence (1776) which said that all men were created equal and entitled to a say in who governed them. Although Ho was aware that these fine words could not always be taken literally and that Americans did not always apply them to non-European peoples, he nevertheless petitioned Wilson for democratic reforms in Vietnam. Wilson ignored him but Ho would never cease to call upon the western democracies to live up to their declared principles. Meanwhile, he was optimistic that his fellow Vietnamese would soon revolt against their French oppressors just as ordinary Russians had apparently rejected their upper-class government. 'It was patriotism and not Communism that originally inspired me,' Ho said later. In 1924 he went to Moscow where he met Soviet leaders such as Stalin, but he found that they were disappointingly uninterested in little Vietnam. Later in the year he visited China where he began to organise Vietnamese students into a revolutionary league, leaving for France when his Chinese Communist friends were persecuted. 'I have become a professional revolutionary,' he told a French friend in 1927.

*A Vietnamese nationalist cartoon from the early 1930s showed peasants driving out French colonial troops.
The peasants shout, 'Wipe out the gang of imperialists, mandarins, capitalists, and big landlords!'*

Meanwhile back home Vietnamese nationalists clashed with their French colonialist oppressors. Believing that the time was now ripe for revolution, Ho established the Indochinese Communist Party in Hong Kong in 1929. He continued travelling throughout the 1930s, carefully observing Communism in China and the Soviet Union. By now he was fluent in Russian, Chinese, French and English, as well as Vietnamese.

In many ways the revolutionary nationalist Ho represented the Vietnam of the future. Vietnam's Emperor Bao Dai collaborated with the hated foreigners and represented the past.

c) Bao Dai - the French Puppet

Bao Dai's late-eighteenth century ancestor had come to power in collaboration with the French. Bao Dai was crowned emperor at the age of 12 in 1925. His French colonial masters sent him to Paris for a French education. Bao Dai returned to Vietnam aged 19. He attempted to govern through a cabinet of nationalists but he lacked the forceful personality necessary to shake off French tutelage. He could not even stand up to his own mother, a formidable harridan addicted to gambling and betel nuts (a sort of Vietnamese chewing gum which rotted and blackened teeth). Powerless and bored, Bao Dai devoted himself to hunting animals and women. An American described him as a 'short, slippery-looking customer rather on the podgy side and freshly dipped in oil' who 'wore a fixed, oily grin that was vaguely reptilian'. When accused of spending too much time watching movies, he said it was in order to improve his English.

During the Second World War Bao Dai exchanged French domination for Japanese domination. Japanese expansionism began in the late nineteenth century and changed the Pacific world. By 1939 Japan dominated Korea, Taiwan and much of coastal China. The outbreak of war in Europe distracted European colonial powers such as France. When Hitler defeated France in June 1940, the Japanese demanded the right to have Japanese soldiers and bases in northern French Indochina (Vietnam). The French had to agree. In July 1941 the Japanese invaded southern Indochina and in December 1941 they attacked the United States and took over the colonial possessions of Britain and America. Exasperated by Bao Dai's collaboration with foreign imperialists, Vietnamese nationalists desperately sought effective leadership. Many looked to Ho Chi Minh to provide it.

In early 1941 Ho finally returned to his native land. He told other nationalists that all Vietnamese should unite to fight both the Japanese and their French collaborators in Indochina. Ho and his friends were both nationalists and Communists. They called their movement the Vietnam Independence League but became more commonly known as the Vietminh. The Vietminh treated ordinary Vietnamese civilians with respect and promised a fairer distribution of wealth and power and freedom from foreigners. It was now that Ho changed his name. His new name of Ho Chi Minh meant 'Bringer of Light'.

2 When and Why Did America Become Involved in Vietnam?

a) Ho's Early Relations With the Americans

One of the main reasons the Americans got involved in Vietnam was their dislike of Ho. It is therefore important to trace the early relationship between Ho and America in order to see whether their enmity was inevitable and justifiable.

Ho was impressed by the military and economic might of the United States, and hoped that he could gain American support for Vietnamese independence. Ho's Vietminh co-operated with the Americans in the fight against the Japanese. Given the trouble that Ho would cause America in years to come, it is ironic that it was probably an American doctor who saved Ho's life in July 1945. A group of Americans had found Ho looking like 'a pile of bones covered with dry yellow skin', suffering from dysentery, malaria and several other tropical diseases for which the doctor gave him treatment. The Americans grew to admire Ho's Vietminh troops and their brilliant General Giap. Ho knew how to flatter Americans. He enlisted their aid in drafting the speech he made before hundreds of thousands of his fellow countrymen on 2 September 1945 after the Japanese surrender. In that speech Ho declared the independence of the Democratic Republic of Vietnam. He began by quoting from the American Declaration of Independence:

1 'All men are created equal. They are endowed by their Creator with certain inalienable rights; among these are Life, Liberty and the pursuit of Happiness.' This immortal statement was made in the Declaration of Independence of the United States of America in 1776 ... The
5 Declaration of the French Revolution made in 1791 ... also states: 'All men are born free and with equal rights ...' Those are undeniable truths ... The French have fled, the Japanese have capitulated, Emperor Bao Dai has abdicated. Our people have broken the chains which for nearly a century have fettered us and have won independence for the
10 Fatherland. The whole Vietnamese people, animated by a common purpose, are determined to fight to the bitter end against any attempt by the French colonialists to reconquer our country. We are convinced that the Allied nations [led by America, Britain and the Soviet Union] have acknowledged the principles of self-determination and equality of
15 nations ... [and] will not refuse to acknowledge the independence of Vietnam ... The entire Vietnamese people are determined to mobilise

all their physical and mental strength, to sacrifice their lives and prop-
erty, in order to safeguard their independence and freedom.

It is difficult to say whether Ho was genuinely optimistic that the
Americans would support him. In the summer of 1941 President
Roosevelt announced that he wanted 'to see sovereign rights and self-
government restored to those who have been forcibly deprived of
them'. During the Second World War, as Ho pointed out in his declaration of independence, Roosevelt frequently repeated these sentiments. In August 1945 General Giap told the Hanoi crowds that
America was a 'good friend', being 'a democracy without territorial
ambitions'. However, at the end of the year, in conversation with Bao
Dai (who had abdicated in favour of Ho and agreed to be Ho's
'supreme adviser') Ho was cynical:

> They [the Americans] are only interested in replacing the French ...
> They want to reorganise our economy in order to control it. They are
> capitalists to the core. All that counts for them is business.

Between October 1945 and February 1946 eight messages from Ho to
Washington went unanswered. Why had America stopped co-oper-
ating with Ho? In order to understand this, we need to look at
American wartime ideas on French Indochina and at the policies and
preoccupations of Roosevelt and Truman.

b) American Ideas About Vietnam During the Second World War

Understanding American involvement in Vietnam necessitates
looking at the history of American interest in that country.
  During their struggle against the Japanese (1941-5) the Americans
had not given much thought to French Indochina. President
Roosevelt was critical of French colonialism but uncertain about what
to advocate for French Indochina after Japan was defeated. In 1942
he wanted to inspire the French to fight against the Germans, so he
talked of allowing France to retain colonies such as Indochina after
the war. However, in 1943 he said that France had 'milked' Indochina
for 100 years and left the Vietnamese people 'worse off than they were
in the beginning', which made him feel that an international trustee-
ship would be the best thing for Indochina. He felt that Indochina
offered strategically important naval bases so he proposed that
America should be one trustee, along with Chiang Kai-shek's China
and the USSR. Soon afterwards he changed his mind again and
suggested that the French could retain Indochina if they promised to
steer it towards independence. Finally, just before his death in 1945,
he offered Indochina to Chiang. Already overburdened with problems, Chiang explained the traditional Vietnamese hatred of China
and politely declined. There are several possible explanations for

Roosevelt's apparent inconsistency over the fate of French Indochina. He tended to think out loud, to test his ideas on people, and to speak to win favour with a particular audience. He was also preoccupied with winning the war: 'I still do not want to get mixed up in any Indochina decision,' he told a colleague on 1 January 1945. 'Action at this time is premature.' The experts in his State Department disagreed amongst themselves and offered him conflicting advice: the Far East division criticised French rule and claimed that unless France allowed self-government in Indochina there would be bloodshed and unrest there for years; the European specialists were pro-French, seeing France as an ally in Europe, and they urged the president to refrain from any policy toward Indochina that might alienate the French.

In April 1945 Roosevelt died in office and was succeeded by Vice-President Harry Truman. Truman sided with the European group in the State Department. He assured the French that America recognised their pre-eminent position in Indochina, while expressing the hope that they would grant more self-government to the Vietnamese. Although American intelligence agents in Hanoi reported to Truman in September 1945 that the traditionally nationalistic Vietnamese were 'determined to maintain their independence even at the cost of their lives', the Truman administration helped restore French rule.

c) Why Truman Aided the French in Indochina

Underlying American interest in the Pacific since the nineteenth century had been America's desire for trade. In addition, Americans believed that opposing ideologies such as Japanese fascism and Soviet Communism threatened the free trade and democratic ideals which were important to American well-being and security. Therefore, America became involved in Vietnam for a mixture of economic and ideological reasons. Individuals were also important. As a new and non-elected president, Truman felt he had to appear tough and decisive in foreign policy. Relatively ignorant about the rest of the world, he relied heavily upon men like Dean Acheson, whom he made Secretary of State in 1949. Acheson believed in standing up to Communists. Truman and Acheson's interpretation of events in Europe and the Far East led to the first significant American commitment to Vietnam. It is therefore necessary to look at those events.

During the Second World War America and her allies had agreed that Chiang's Chinese Nationalists would take the surrender of the Japanese forces in northern Vietnam, while the British would take their surrender in southern Vietnam. Japan surrendered in August 1945 and the Chinese and British moved into Vietnam as agreed. Vietnam was in chaos. Japanese troops waited to be returned home, Chinese Nationalists pillaged the north, Ho declared Vietnamese independence and struggled for power with other Vietnamese factions. In September 1945 some Vietminh clashed with French soldiers released by the Japanese in Saigon and some consider this the outbreak of the first Vietnam war. Fighting between Ho's Vietminh and the French escalated and increasing numbers of French troops were transported to Indochina by the pro-colonialist British. America went along with this because it feared disorder in Indochina might create a vacuum into which China would flow. Ho had similar fears. Despairing of gaining foreign recognition of Vietnamese independence, he preferred the French to the Chinese. The French he said,

> are weak. Colonialism is dying. The white man is finished in Asia. But if the Chinese stay now, they will never go. I prefer to sniff French shit for five years than eat Chinese shit for the rest of my life.

Chiang's Chinese Nationalist forces soon returned home to deal with the Chinese Communists, but fighting between the French and the Vietminh continued throughout 1946. Keen to compensate for her humiliation during the Second World War and to retain wealthy southern Vietnam, France was reluctant to give in and get out altogether. The French appealed to a sympathetic President Truman for aid, cleverly maintaining that Ho was part of a worldwide Communist conspiracy orchestrated by Moscow and likely to lead to Soviet domination everywhere. America feared and loathed Communism and had long been suspicious of the Soviet Union. Although the USA and USSR were wartime allies against Germany (1941-5) their alliance was always uneasy. Stalin's 'liberation' of eastern Europe developed into outright Soviet domination during 1945-9 and, when coupled with Soviet moves in Iran and the eastern Mediterranean, convinced the Truman administration that the Communists must be 'contained' (for the containment doctrine, see the Cold War volume in this series). By 1947 the Truman administration felt that Ho was probably a puppet of the Kremlin. This was the main reason why America gave increasing support to the French in Vietnam. Some State Department specialists feared that the administration was over-simplifying matters and during 1948 pointed out that Ho had made friendly gestures to America and that the Vietnamese Communists were NOT subservient to the Kremlin, but the general atmosphere in early Cold War America was not conducive to such subtleties of analysis.

In 1949 Acheson said that it was 'irrelevant' to ask whether Ho was 'as much nationalist as Commie' for 'all Stalinists in colonial areas are nationalists'. This American conviction that what was at stake in Vietnam was the expansion of Communism was eventually to embroil America in a bloody and disastrous war there. However, the distinction between Ho's nationalism and Communism WAS relevant. Ho was always a nationalist first. Stalin recognised this. Americans did not.

Late in 1949 Mao Zedong's Communists took over China. Under attack from the Republicans for having 'lost' China and fearing further Communist expansion in Asia, Acheson persuaded Truman to give more money to help French forces in Indochina. US fears of a worldwide Communist offensive seemed justified when Ho (having failed to obtain American recognition in exchange for a promise of neutrality in the Cold War) persuaded China and the Soviets to recognise his Democratic Republic of Vietnam in January 1950. In the next month Senator Joseph McCarthy began whipping many Americans into an anti-Communist frenzy. When Communist North Korea attacked South Korea in 1950 the United States mobilised the United Nations in a war to halt Communist aggression in the Far East. According to America's military leaders, the Joint Chiefs of Staff (JCS), the world balance of power was at stake in Southeast Asia, an area full of strategically vital materials, where American allies such as Japan and Australia might be vulnerable to Communist attack. When Chinese troops poured into Korea, American fears of Chinese expansionism were confirmed. In this situation and atmosphere it is not surprising that the Truman administration concluded that Indochina must not be allowed to fall into Communist hands.

The administration also concluded that the French were invaluable allies against Communism in both Indochina and Europe, and therefore deserving of American assistance. Acheson and Truman were very conscious that France was important to the stability of the western alliance in Europe and to NATO. When France clearly linked the issues of Franco-American co-operation in Europe with American aid in Indochina, it served to confirm the US belief that they must become more involved in that region. Franco-American relations were not always smooth: some Americans in Vietnam saw the French rather than the Vietminh as the enemy! By 1954 the Americans were more convinced than the French of the importance of Vietnam in the global struggle against Communism and America was paying nearly 80 per cent of the French bill for Indochina. Truman had given over $2 billion to the French war effort and $50 million for economic and technical aid to the Vietnamese people.

The French recognised Vietnam's 'independence' under their feeble puppet emperor, Bao Dai, on whose behalf they kept control of Vietnam's army, finance and foreign policy. Bao Dai expended most of his limited energy in a long-running dispute with the French High Commissioner over which of them should use the presidential palace in Saigon! He told an American diplomat that after his brief co-operation with Ho and exile he had returned to Vietnam only because the French had promised independence. Near to tears he asked: 'This independence, what is it? Where is it? Do you see it?' All this caused anxious voices within the Truman administration. Some criticised Bao Dai and feared that France and America were being distracted from the more important issue of European defence against Communism by this involvement in Indochina. One State Department Far Eastern specialist admitted that 'the trouble is that none of us knows enough about Indochina'. A Defence Department official warned in November 1950 that America was becoming dangerously and deeply involved:

> we are gradually increasing our stake in the outcome of the struggle ... we are dangerously close to the point of being so deeply committed that we may find ourselves completely committed even to direct intervention. These situations, unfortunately, have a way of snowballing.

That official was right. Fearful of the Communist governments of Russia and China, and believing that Ho was their puppet, the Truman administration had got the United States involved in French-dominated Vietnam.

Summary Diagram
Vietnam and Foreigners to 1953

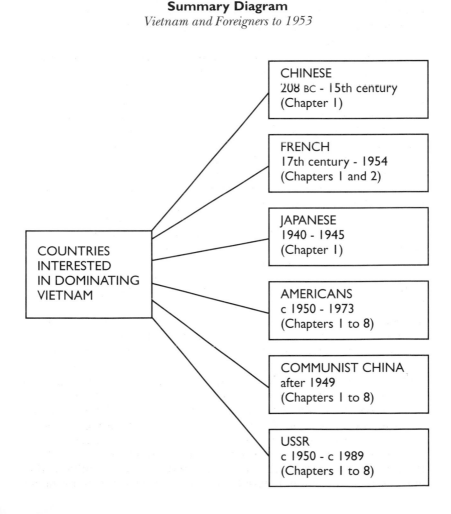

COUNTRIES
INTERESTED
IN DOMINATING
VIETNAM

CHINESE
208 BC - 15th century
(Chapter 1)

FRENCH
17th century - 1954
(Chapters 1 and 2)

JAPANESE
1940 - 1945
(Chapter 1)

AMERICANS
c 1950 - 1973
(Chapters 1 to 8)

COMMUNIST CHINA
after 1949
(Chapters 1 to 8)

USSR
c 1950 - c 1989
(Chapters 1 to 8)

This chapter contains a great deal of background knowledge upon which it is unlikely that you will ever be directly questioned, so you will probably summarise much of it in the form of your own date list. When you make your notes on this chapter the issues you should be thinking about are (i) why it was difficult for foreigners to dominate Vietnam and (ii) why the Truman administration got involved there. Making your notes follow the textbook order is the easiest way to take notes, and is often the safest if you are relatively unused to thinking independently. However, some students recognise the advantages of reshaping the notes, altering the order and providing their own sub-headings, as this makes them think more about what they are writing. For example, you could make notes assessing the impact of all the different countries (China, France, Japan, Britain and America) on Vietnam.

There are several types of source-based questions that you will probably be asked to work upon. In this and the succeeding chapters there will be 'model answers' to each question type.

Specimen Question
A 'comprehension' question checks whether you understand particular words, phrases, arguments or points of view in a document, for example:
a) Look at Ho Chi Minh's declaration of independence on pages 10-11 and explain the following references:
(i) 'Bao Dai' (1 mark)
(ii) 'the Japanese have capitulated' (1 mark)
b) How does Ho make his declaration appealing to Americans? (2 marks)

Specimen Answer
Suitable answers would be:
a) (i) Bao Dai was the Vietnamese emperor who, like his ancestors, collaborated with foreigners who dominated Vietnam, whether French (1925-40) or Japanese (1940-5). [When asked about an individual for one mark, you do not want to write too much, but if you can put several pieces of information into one sentence you should cover everything the examiner is likely to expect.]
(ii) Ho spoke in early September 1945. In August the Japanese had surrendered to America and her allies Britain and China.
b) Ho flatters the Americans by quoting from their declaration of independence and calling it that 'immortal statement.' He implies that the Vietnamese have been influenced by and learned

from America and having thus made the declaration appeal to Americans, hopes thereby to gain American support. [It is always useful to:

a) quote briefly from the source to show and prove what you are talking about, and

b) to repeat the keywords of the question to keep yourself on the right track and to show the examiner that you are answering his particular question. Here, for example, the phrase 'appeal to Americans' echoes the question.]

Now attempt to answer the following set of questions on your own. If you find any of them too difficult at this stage, return to them during revision.

1. The Vietnamese desire for independence

Look at the Vietnamese cartoon on page 8, Ho's declaration of independence on pages 10-11, and his comments to Bao Dai on page 11. Answer the following questions.

a) (i) What was a mandarin? (1 mark)

(ii) Explain the phrase 'broke the chains which for nearly a century have fettered us'. (1 mark)

(iii) What did Ho mean by 'self-determination' and why did he use that particular phrase? (2 marks)

b) Which Vietnamese sentiment is common to all three sources? Illustrate your answer by specific references to the sources. (3 marks)

c) In what ways does the tone of Ho's comments to Bao Dai differ from his tone in the declaration of independence? Account for the difference. (5 marks)

d) How useful is the cartoon to a historian trying to understand Ho's beliefs and popularity? (5 marks)

e) Using the sources and your own background knowledge, suggest reasons why so many Vietnamese nationalists became Communists. (8 marks)

3 Eisenhower and Two Vietnams

A century of French involvement in Indochina ended in 1954, at a conference held at Geneva in Switzerland. Laos, Cambodia and a divided Vietnam emerged from this conference. Truman's successor President Eisenhower became the sponsor of the southern part of Vietnam, while Ho Chi Minh led the north. This chapter will explain how the two Vietnams were created and why Eisenhower's America helped create a new state called South Vietnam. This should allow you to make judgements about the extent to which Eisenhower was responsible for American involvement in Vietnam and whether or not that involvement was wise. The chapter begins with a brief study of how the Vietnamese defeated the French which helps to explain how they were able to defeat the Americans years later.

1 Ho, Giap and the French Failure in Indochina

Eisenhower inherited Truman's commitment to the French and their puppet emperor, Bao Dai. He continued to finance the French military effort and the extravagant emperor whose other sources of revenue included gambling casinos, brothels and opium dens in Saigon. In late 1951 a US official said Bao Dai's government:

1   is in no sense the servant of the people. It has no grass roots. It there-
    fore has no appeal whatsoever to the masses ... Revolution will
    continue and Ho Chi Minh will remain a popular hero so long as 'inde-
    pendence' leaders with French support are simply native mandarins
5   who are succeeding foreign mandarins.

Ho Chi Minh compared the struggle between the French and the Vietminh to a fight between an elephant and a grasshopper. Although the French seemed more powerful, Ho's Vietminh proved elusive and determined. 'You can kill ten of my men for every one I kill of yours,' Ho told one Frenchman, 'but even at those odds, you will lose and I will win.' The French had more men and materials but Vietminh guerrilla tactics utilised the physical geography of the country. The Vietminh would make surprise attacks then retreat to western Vietnam's jungle and mountains which were enveloped by monsoon mist for half the year. The Chinese supplied Ho with weapons, including the latest American ones, captured from Chiang's defeated Nationalists. Most important of all, the Vietminh fought for an inspiring cause, a free and more egalitarian Vietnam. Many were as fanatical as their brilliant military commander Vo Nguyen Giap.

Giap's father was a mandarin who had participated in anti-French uprisings in the 1880s. Both he and one of his daughters were 'subversives' who died in French prisons. Like Ho, Giap admired French culture but loathed French colonialism. The French had Giap on their list of revolutionary nationalists from the time he was 13 years old. He attended Vietnam's only university, at Hanoi, and in 1937 joined the Indochinese Communist Party. Another of his sisters was shot by the French for being a Communist. Giap felt Communism, with its emphasis on co-operation and sharing, fitted in with Vietnamese traditions and was therefore appropriate for Vietnam. He read widely on Vietnamese history, Communism, and military strategy. In 1940 he met Ho and impressed him with his military knowledge. Giap and Ho collected dedicated individuals known as cadres around them. By 1944 Giap had trained several hundred military cadres. Hiding from the French in the jungles, they were sometimes forced to survive on insects, roots and tree bark. In true Communist fashion, all had to contribute to community life in these years: Giap became chief dish washer, having been voted out of the chef's job. In 1943 the death of his wife at the hands of the French added to his fanaticism. From 1944 he commanded the Vietnamese Liberation Army. His Vietminh forces numbered around 5,000. At this time, he got on well with the Americans who gave him his first modern weapons for use against the Japanese. He made pro-American references in his speech on 'independence day' after the Japanese defeat. During 1946 he continued to improve the armaments of the 5,000 strong army of the Democratic Republic of Vietnam. However, Ho was alarmed when Giap had a public and passionate love affair with a famous dancer, attended night clubs, and began wearing fashionable western dress. He quickly introduced Giap to a serious and well-educated woman from a distinguished family. Giap married her and the embarrassing criticisms ceased. In November 1946 the Vietminh officially declared war on the French. Giap improved military training and set out plans for revolutionary war. He would start with guerrilla warfare to wear down the enemy, then slowly move to set-piece battles as his army grew stronger. Like Ho, Giap paid great attention to winning over the ordinary people.

Mao's 1949 triumph transformed the situation. Giap and Ho gained diplomatic recognition, more armaments, advice, and sanctuary in China if Vietnamese soldiers were in trouble. By 1952 Giap commanded over a quarter of a million regular soldiers and a militia nearing two million. Each army division was supported by 40,000 porters carrying rice or ammunition along jungle trails and over mountain passes. Giap's soldiers willingly suffered for their country and their freedom:

1   We had to cross mountains and jungles, marching at night and sleeping by day to avoid enemy bombing. We slept in foxholes [bomb craters], or simply alongside the trail. We each carried a rifle, ammunition and hand grenades, and our packs contained a blanket, a mosquito net and a
5   change of clothes. We each had a week's supply of rice, which we refilled at depots along the way. We ate greens and bamboo shoots, picked in

the jungle, and occasionally villagers would give us a bit of meat. By then I had been in the Vietminh for nine years, and I was accustomed to it.

Units held self-criticism sessions, during which errors were admitted and forgiven. Soldiers followed set rules when dealing with civilians: BE POLITE; BE FAIR; RETURN EVERYTHING BORROWED; DO NOT BULLY; DO NOT FRATERNISE WITH WOMEN; TRY NOT TO CAUSE DAMAGE AND IF YOU DO, PAY FOR IT. Ho's fairer redistribution of land, and educational and health care programmes also served to win over the Vietnamese peasantry.

While Ho and Giap went from strength to strength, the French had problems. They tried what they called 'yellowing' their army (enlisting native Vietnamese) but did not trust these new recruits and gave them little responsibility. In France itself, many people were beginning to lose heart and interest in Indochina. Just at that time a great military struggle was taking place at Dien Bien Phu.

2 The Geneva Conference on Indochina, 1954

a) The Call for an International Conference

While the Vietminh and French soldiers prepared for what both rightly thought would be a crucial clash at Dien Bien Phu, the changing international situation increased enthusiasm for a conference on Indochina. An armistice had finally ended three years of bitter fighting in Korea, so the time seemed ripe to try to end the fighting in French Indochina. Stalin had died and the new Soviet leaders appeared keen to decrease Cold War tension. In France many were tiring of the struggle and/or were aware of worldwide expectation that the war ought to be brought to an end. Communist China favoured negotiations because it wanted to forestall American involvement in Indochina and it judged that participation in the peace talks would gain it increased international recognition and respectability. Not everyone was enthusiastic about negotiations. Ho Chi Minh and the Vietnamese Communists were clearly winning the struggle for Vietnam. They feared and distrusted the French and did not expect to gain by talking to them. Bao Dai's new prime minister Ngo Dinh Diem feared and distrusted both the French and Ho and did not want to negotiate with either of them. Diem simply wanted the French out of Vietnam and a chance to concentrate upon defeating the Communists. The Eisenhower administration in the United States feared that in their eagerness to get out of Vietnam the French might concede too much to the Communists.

The Chinese and Russians put great pressure on Ho to negotiate but even before he said 'yes' the Russians agreed to a conference. Talks on the future of French Indochina were to begin on 8 May 1954 at Geneva. Meanwhile the struggle for Dien Bien Phu continued. The French had decided to concentrate their efforts on Dien Bien Phu, but it was an odd place to make a great stand. It was situated in a valley, which Giap's forces bombarded from the surrounding high ground. Despite (or because of) the comfort afforded by 18 prostitutes and 49,000 bottles of wine, the French garrison there was doing badly.

b) Dien Bien Phu - the Debate Over American Intervention

Not long before the showdown at Dien Bien Phu, Eisenhower had given the French $385 million dollars worth of armaments for an offensive against the Vietminh. In return the French promised to grant Indochina greater independence. There was a considerable debate raging within the Eisenhower administration about the extent to which America should be involved in Vietnam. Many questions were being asked. Was Southeast Asia vital to US security? If it was, should America get involved in Indochina? If it did, should US involvement in Indochina take the form of financial aid to the French, US military advisers assisting the French, US air and/or sea support for the French, or the sending of US ground troops to Indochina? Did the US have enough troops to make a difference in Indochina? Was victory possible in Indochina in conjunction with the French or if America were there alone? Was America willing to risk a clash with China over intervention in Indochina? How much was America willing to do without allied (including UN) support?

Like most of the men in his administration, Eisenhower believed that Southeast Asia WAS vital to US security. However, he was more moderate than many in his views on what America should do there. He considered it easier and cheaper to pay other countries to help defend America: Communism threatened America and the French were fighting Communism, so it was better to pay the French to fight Communism than to send American boys to do it. When the French got into trouble early in 1954 Eisenhower responded to their pleas for extra help by sending US bombers accompanied by 200 American technicians. Eisenhower told Congress in February 1954 that he disliked putting these Americans in danger but that 'we must not lose Asia'. Eisenhower had put the first American personnel into Vietnam. In March the situation at Dien Bien Phu was beginning to look hopeless so France requested a US air strike against the Vietminh in order to strengthen the French negotiating position at Geneva. While American schoolchildren prayed for the French to defeat the atheist Communists, Eisenhower gave the request serious consideration.

Eisenhower was concerned about Vietnam and Dien Bien Phu for several reasons. French strength was being drained away in Vietnam and he wanted France to be a strong NATO member to help defend Western Europe against the Soviet threat. The French threatened to be unhelpful about European defence arrangements and to get out of Indochina unless America aided them there. In the presidential election campaign Eisenhower had rejected the Democratic policy of containment of Communism and had advocated liberation of Communist countries. As yet he had not 'liberated' a single soul from Communism. Eisenhower knew that Truman's popularity had suffered greatly because he had 'lost' China and he did not want the Democrats to say he had 'lost' Vietnam. In a speech broadcast on TV and radio in March 1954, Secretary of State John Foster Dulles made it clear that the administration feared Chinese expansion in Indochina. He pointed out that the Vietminh were trained and equipped by the Chinese. Most important of all, Eisenhower felt that the loss of Vietnam to Communism would affect the global balance of power. He feared that if the US allowed Vietnam to fall to Communism other Southeast Asian countries would follow. At a press conference in April 1954 Eisenhower explained that Vietnam was vitally important to America.

> 1 You have the specific value of a locality in its production of materials [rice, rubber, coal, iron ore] that the world needs. You have the possibility that many human beings pass under a dictatorship that is inimical to the free world. You have the broader considerations that might follow
> 5 what you would call the 'falling domino' principle ... You have a row of dominoes set up, you knock over the first one, and what will happen to the last one is the certainty that it will go over very quickly.

Eisenhower privately said that 'in certain areas at least we cannot afford to let Moscow gain another bit of territory' and that Dien Bien Phu might be such a place. He briefly toyed with the idea of a lightning American air strike - in unmarked planes because 'we would have to deny it for ever'.

Not every influential American agreed that something should be done about Vietnam. Some disliked the domino theory, doubting whether the loss of a relatively small country to Communism would cause the loss of others. Some of the military and the Secretary of Defence felt that Indochina was 'devoid of decisive military objectives' and that any US intervention there would be pointless, 'a serious diversion of limited US capabilities'. One vice-admiral insisted that 'partial' involvement through air and sea forces alone would be a delusion. 'One cannot go over Niagara Falls in a barrel only slightly,' he said. Whilst he was commander of NATO Eisenhower himself had said that 'no military victory is possible in that kind of theatre' and in the early 1960s he would write in his memoirs that 'the jungles of Indochina would have swallowed up division after division of US troops'. He pointed out the dangerous possibility that the US could find itself fighting Communists everywhere and felt he could not put US troops on the Asian mainland again just one year after he had gained massive popularity by getting them out of Korea. Even had he wanted to send US troops, there were none readily available. The Republicans' 'new look' defence policy emphasised nuclear weaponry at the expense of manpower. Many Americans were uncertain about the wisdom of being too closely entangled with the French in Indochina. The French themselves disliked the American conditions for involvement. France did not want to grant total independence to Vietnam and then carry on fighting there under a US commander. Eisenhower wrote in his memoirs that 'the strongest reason of all' for America to stay out

> is the fact that among all the powerful nations ... the United States is the only one with a tradition of anti-colonialism ... an asset of incalculable value ... The moral position of the United States was more to be guarded than ... all of Indochina.

He clearly recognised the danger of replacing French colonialism with American colonialism. Perhaps more importantly, Eisenhower and Dulles tried but failed to get the British support that Congress required before they would approve American military intervention. Prime Minister Churchill said the struggle was not winnable and might trigger off World War Three. Ironically, one unenthusiastic senator was Lyndon Johnson. Faced with all this uncertainty, Eisenhower decided against direct American intervention in Vietnam. Without American intervention, the French were doomed to defeat at Dien Bien Phu. That defeat would ensure that the French government and people were finally ready to give up and get out of Indochina.

c) The Geneva Conference

On 7 May 1954 the Vietminh raised their red flag over Dien Bien Phu. The next day delegations representing France, Bao Dai, the Vietminh, Cambodia, Laos, the United States, the Soviet Union, the People's Republic of China and Great Britain assembled in Geneva to discuss ending the war in Indochina. Each delegation had different aims. Ho's Vietminh aimed to take over as much of Vietnam as possible and get foreigners out. Bao Dai sought Vietnamese independence and an easy life. The French wanted to end their colonial war while trying to retain some influence in Indochina. America sought to contain Communism in Southeast Asia and to avoid elections in Vietnam, knowing Ho Chi Minh would win. America rejected the idea of Communists in the government of Vietnam, and hoped for a united non-Communist Vietnam. The Chinese aimed at peace in Indochina to keep foreigners away from China's borders while she recovered from civil war. China also wanted to appear impressive and to gain diplomatic recognition and trade contacts. The Soviets aimed to divide both the French and Americans, and Ho and the Chinese. They were anxious to defuse troublesome situations that could hurt the USSR. The British wanted to stop the advance of Communism and prevent a wider war.

Occasionally and fittingly the proceedings resembled a French farce. Prime Minister Zhou Enlai of China was keen to make a dramatic impact. He arrived complete with the largest retinue (200) and Chinese antiques and carpets to decorate his lavish lodgings, all of which elicited snide remarks from his comrades from the Soviet Union. The Vietminh studiously ignored the delegations of Bao Dai, Cambodia, Laos and France. Dulles refused to shake hands with Zhou and advised Eisenhower not to smile for press photographs whilst in the company of Communists but unfortunately the president failed to restrain his famous grin. The French were impatient with the American refusal to recognise the Chinese, while the Americans found the French secretive and the British weak. The British Foreign Secretary said he had never known a conference like it. It is not surprising that it did not produce a durable settlement. The Americans were unwilling to commit themselves to any agreements made, partly to avoid giving any concessions to the Communists, partly to avoid being linked to any settlement that was unlikely to work. Back in Washington the intervention debate was raging again but Congress proved unwilling to intervene.

At first no agreement seemed possible at Geneva, but then a new French government, which was determined to settle the affair, came to power. Meanwhile, Zhou was equally determined to gain a settlement that would keep the Americans out of Indochina and as far away from China as possible. Zhou was willing to sacrifice comrade Ho in the interests of China, especially when it made him and his country look peace-loving, moderate and statesmanlike.

d) The Agreements at Geneva (1954)

The Vietminh, in effect represented by Zhou, agreed with France that
1. There would be Communist rule in the north of Vietnam while Bao Dai and his new Prime Minister, Diem, would govern the south. Ho's Vietminh would have to give up the territory which they occupied south of the 17th parallel (the line of partition between north and south Vietnam was fixed at the latitude of 17 degrees north of the Equator, known as the 17th parallel).
2. The French forces would withdraw from the north and Ho's Vietminh forces from the south. There would be a truce between them.
3. There would be democratic elections for a single Vietnamese government in two years' time. Vietnam would then be unified.
4. Neither the northern nor the southern Vietnamese were to make any military alliances with foreign powers, nor were they to allow foreign military bases in their territories. The French would remain in the south only in order to help prepare for the elections in two years' time.

These Geneva agreements were highly significant. While they

Redrawing the map at the Geneva Conference (1954).

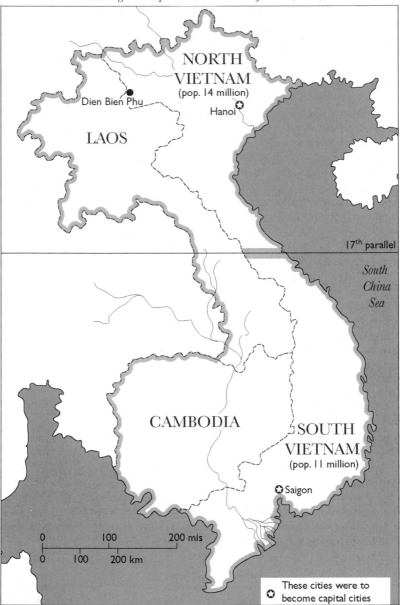

French Indochina consisted of what Americans would come to know as Vietnam, Laos and Cambodia. At Geneva, Vietnam was temporarily (supposedly) divided along the 17th parallel into a Communist North (under Ho) and a non-Communist South (under Bao Dai and Diem). Elections would (supposedly) be held in 1956 to reunite the country. Laos and Cambodia gained independence.

appeared to recognise Vietnamese aspirations, they actually reflected great power wishes. Ho had no choice but to accept a settlement which forced the Vietminh to retreat. He needed time for consolidation in the North. He also needed Soviet aid and the Soviets wanted peace. He believed there would be nationwide elections in 1956 and knew that as the most popular Vietnamese national figure he was virtually certain to win. Eisenhower later admitted that Ho would have won 80 per cent of the vote in a fair election. The negotiations showed that Communist China and the Soviet Union were not uncompromisingly supportive of Ho and his Democratic Republic of Vietnam. They had urged Ho to retreat. The United States was significantly slow to pick up and/or exploit such divisions within the Communist world. Dulles knew there were Sino-Soviet tensions yet did not use them to advantage at Geneva. The cease-fire in Vietnam was between the French and the Vietminh - not between the Vietminh and any South Vietnamese government. New premier Diem of South Vietnam rejected the agreements as they put half of Vietnam under Communist control. He rightly predicted that 'another more deadly war' lay ahead. The Eisenhower administration refused to sign the Geneva agreements, saying 'the United States has not itself been a party to or bound by the decisions taken', and warned that America would view 'any renewal of aggression' with 'grave concern'. American chose to misinterpret the temporary cease-fire line of the 17th parallel as a permanent division between two states, a northern one which was Communist and a southern one which was friendly. The Geneva settlement and Vietnam had become victims of the Cold War.

3 Two Vietnams

After the Geneva conference, Ho and the Communists governed North Vietnam (from Hanoi) while Diem governed South Vietnam (from Saigon). Like all Vietnamese nationalists, Ho and Diem would have preferred a united Vietnam. One great question was whether either of them had the necessary skill and support to bring about national unification. Another great question was whether the Vietnamese would at last be able to decide their own destiny without foreign interference.

a) Ngo Dinh Diem - Background

The short, plump and chain-smoking Diem usually wore the white sharkskin suits that were a status symbol for Vietnamese officials. His ancestors came from central Vietnam where they had been converted to Christianity by Portuguese missionaries in the seventeenth century. Generations of them had served as mandarins at the imperial Vietnamese court. Diem was the third of the Ngo family's six sons.

The young Diem had considered becoming a priest but had decided that it would require too much self-discipline. As it turned out, the delicate-featured Diem never married and lived a more monk-like life than his older brother who was a worldly archbishop of the Catholic church. Trained in a French school for Vietnamese bureaucrats, Diem successfully continued the family tradition of government service until he clashed with his French masters in 1933. A nationalist, he resented French unwillingness to give the Vietnamese any real power. Diem skulked around his mother's home for the next decade. He had high hopes of the Japanese allowing Vietnam to declare its independence during the Second World War but they rejected his ideas. A few months after the Vietminh shot his brother, Diem met Ho Chi Minh. Ho asked Diem to join his government and the fight for independence and a better life for the people of Vietnam. Diem replied that Ho's followers were murderers, and that he would fight for the freedom of the people in his own way. Subsequently some Communists criticised Ho for letting Diem go at this point.

In 1950 Diem went to the US where he helped at a seminary for training priests. Disdainful of material comforts, he willingly scrubbed floors. He also met prominent American Catholics such as Senators John Kennedy and Mike Mansfield.

Meanwhile Bao Dai was living on the French riviera with a wife, a mistress, and a variety of French prostitutes who kept him occupied in between visits to the gambling casinos. Bao Dai thought that the American contacts might make Diem useful, so in 1954 he made Diem his prime minister. By that time the vast majority of Vietnamese nationalists with leadership qualities were members of the Vietminh. Any non-Communist nationalists with potential had either been killed by the French or the Vietminh or had given up political activities. Diem thus slid into a leadership vacuum.

b) Diem and the Americans

According to the Geneva agreements, the French were supposed to stay in south Vietnam to enforce the cease-fire until the nationwide elections were held in July 1956. Diem, whom the French prime minister described as incapable and mad, rejected the idea of nation-wide elections because he knew Ho would win. Diem decided to turn his back on the French and to rely instead on the Americans who within weeks of the Geneva conference had pledged him their support.

Diem and his American patrons agreed that the Communist menace must be halted and that one way to do this was to build a stable, non-Communist South Vietnamese state. Eisenhower felt that Ho had triumphed at Geneva and that the United States had to do something to 'restore its prestige in the Far East'. Dulles therefore masterminded the Southeast Asia Treaty Organisation (SEATO) which combined America, Britain, France, Australia, New Zealand and Pakistan in a defensive alliance. SEATO members agreed to protect South Vietnam, Cambodia and Laos under a separate protocol - a transparent American device to circumvent the Genevan agreement which had said that the Vietnamese must not enter into foreign alliances nor allow foreign troops on their soil. From the beginning, however, the Americans were not entirely happy with their new South Vietnamese ally. According to Vice-President Richard Nixon, the problem was that 'the [South] Vietnamese lacked the ability to conduct a war by themselves or govern themselves'. With his high-pitched voice and capacity for endless talking rather than listening, Diem did not impress those Americans to whom he gave audience. Dulles admitted that America supported Diem 'because we knew of no one better': he was simply the best of a bad bunch. The leaders of America's armed forces, the Joint Chiefs of Staff (JCS), were unenthusiastic about involvement with Diem, believing that his government was unstable. Although Dulles contended that helping Diem train his army would make his government stable, a trusted general whom Eisenhower sent to Saigon reported that Diem's regime was hopeless. Another old friend of Eisenhower's doubted whether the US could make 'a synthetic strong man' out of Diem. The Eisenhower administration nearly withdrew their support but Diem's effective action against Bao Dai and other non-Communists opponents halted them. Diem held an election in South Vietnam, now clearly a separate state. Those voting against him were punished: some were held down to have pepper sauce poured into their nostrils. Diem claimed 98.2 per cent of the vote, rejecting American proposals that 60 or 70 per cent were more credible figures. Out of 450,000 registered voters in Saigon, Diem claimed 605,025 had voted for him! Through a combination of force, fraud and friendship with America, Diem appeared to have made himself undisputed leader of the new state of South Vietnam.

The Eisenhower administration now increased aid to Diem, giving him hundreds of millions of dollars and advice on politics, land reform and covert operations against the Vietminh. American recommendations included sabotage and the recruitment of fortune tellers to predict doom under Communism. America had helped transport around one million Vietnamese from the north to the south. Most of the refugees were Catholic and (initially) supportive of Diem, but their arrival made Diem even less popular amongst the predominantly Buddhist southerners.

Diem visited America in 1957 when Eisenhower praised him as the 'miracle man' of Asia. Unfortunately Diem's belief in his own infallibility and rectitude was so strengthened by such words that when Americans advised him that his repressive and unpopular administration needed to reform to survive, Diem dug his heels in and did nothing. His government had become a family operation and while

Diem in thoughtful pose in his Saigon palace

Diem (centre left) with his brother Nhu (rear left), his brother the archbishop (rear right), and his sister-in-law Madame Nhu (centre)

Diem himself lived frugally, his family squabbled amongst themselves in their struggle to get rich. Diem favoured the fellow Catholics from the north and the wealthy landowner class. He never appealed to the ordinary people as Ho did. Like the Americans who supported him, Diem did not understand the appeal of the Vietminh. He simply saw them as rebels and failed to comprehend how their ideas about greater economic equality could win so many peasant hearts. Diem disliked meeting his people and only reluctantly toured South Vietnam at the behest of his American patrons who rightly feared that unlike 'Uncle Ho' he lacked the common touch.

c) Support For Ho and Communism

In many ways Ho's regime in the north was as unpleasant as that of Diem in the south. Ho's Communists liquidated thousands of land-lords and opponents and even loyal Vietminh by mistake. In 1956 Ho's soldiers had to put down a revolt: 6,000 peasants were killed or deported. Subsequently Ho and Giap admitted having wrongfully resorted to terror. On the other hand, Ho's regime often won the hearts of the people in a way that Diem's never did. Joseph Alsop was one of the few Americans who had toured rural south Vietnam when it was still occupied by the Vietminh. He wrote about his 1954 travels for the *New Yorker* in 1955:

1   I would like to be able to report - I had hoped to be able to report - that on that long, slow canal trip to Vinh Binh [Mekong Delta] I saw all the signs of misery and oppression that have made my visits to East Germany like nightmare journeys to 1984 [a reference to the descrip-
5   tions of a totalitarian state in George Orwell's novel *1984*]. But it was not so.
    At first it was difficult for me, as it is for any Westerner, to conceive of a Communist government's genuinely 'serving the people'. I could hardly imagine a Communist government that was also a popular
10   government and almost a democratic government. But this is just the sort of government the palm-hut state actually was while the struggle with the French continued. The Vietminh could not possibly have carried on the resistance for one year, let alone nine years, without the people's strong, united support.

Many southerners remained quietly loyal to Ho after Vietnam was divided in 1954. A large number of southern peasants disliked both the corrupt regime of Diem and the Communists, but many began to turn to the latter.

Before 1959 Ho had discouraged supporters in the south from attacking Diem's regime. Hanoi wanted to be seen to be abiding by the Geneva agreements and was bitterly divided about whether consolidation in the North should take priority over liberation of the South. This gave Diem the opportunity to arrest and execute many southern Communist activists whose numbers dropped from around 10,000 in 1955 to nearer 2,000 by 1959. That forced the South's Communists into open revolt. By 1960 Hanoi had decided to give liberation equal priority to consolidation. Diem responded by concentrating even more upon military solutions. From 1960 Ho's southern supporters called themselves the National Liberation Front but Diem called them Vietcong (VC), which meant Vietnamese Communists. One of the great Vietnam war debates concerns the southern insurgents. Was the opposition to Diem from indigenous southerners who had always remained in the South, or from southerners who had moved North after Geneva and now returned? Or were they primarily indigenous northerners? Were they orchestrated by Hanoi? There is an element of truth in all these suggestions. One thing is indisputable: the level of violence and disruption increased dramatically in South Vietnam from 1958 onwards. Diem responded by relocating peasants to army-protected villages called agrovilles. The peasants hated forced, expensive removals from their homes, lands and sacred ancestral tombs. Dissatisfaction with Diem's regime was ever-increasing. In 1960 eighteen prominent Vietnamese nationalists petitioned Diem for moderate reform but he became even more repressive in response.

By this time Diem had received over a billion dollars from the Eisenhower administration. 'We bet pretty heavily on him,' said Eisenhower, while Senator Kennedy described Diem as 'our offspring'. One exasperated US official in Saigon described Diem as 'a puppet who pulled his own strings - and ours as well'. While many knowledgeable Americans warned from the first that the struggle could not be won with Diem in power, others disagreed. Diem's American supporters were often those who saw the conflict in Vietnam in simple military terms, believing that Diem's battles were against unpopular Communists and could be won simply by pouring in more military aid and money ($7 billion between 1955 and 1961). The problem was that the Communists had a fair amount of popular support in South Vietnam and that Diem had to deal with so much non-Communist opposition. Even his army contained opponents, some of whom unsuccessfully rebelled against him in 1960. By 1961 America was supporting a very unpopular regime in South Vietnam.

4 Assessment of Eisenhower's Policy Towards Vietnam

While campaigning for the presidency Eisenhower had emphasised the importance of liberating people from Communism and by those self-imposed standards he had failed. North Vietnam became a Communist state during his presidency. However, recent historians generally do not consider him a failure because it is the American involvement in Vietnam that they consider disastrous. They tend to judge presidents by the extent to which they got America committed. Eisenhower did not send thousands of American troops to Vietnam as Johnson did, so Eisenhower is judged to have been relatively successful in dealing with Vietnam. As we recap on what he thought and did about Vietnam, you might disagree.

Eisenhower inherited a limited involvement in Vietnam. Truman had financially aided the French in their struggle to retain influence in Vietnam because he believed that Vietnam was important in the Cold War. All members of the Eisenhower administration agreed that Vietnam was important. Some (including Vice-President Nixon and, possibly, Dulles) were even willing to use atomic bombs to help the French there but Eisenhower said,

> You boys must be crazy. We can't use those awful things against Asians for the second time in less than ten years. My God.

Eisenhower deserves credit for rejecting the atomic option. He recognised that the use of atomic bombs would probably lead to conflict with the Soviets and China. Nonetheless, Eisenhower's administration made Vietnam even more important than Truman's had. Some historians praise him for refusing to send Americans into combat in Vietnam. His memoirs suggest he realised this was militarily and politically unwise. However, it must be remembered that he gave a great deal of support to the French attempts at a military solution. Furthermore, it was probably only congressional leaders and the reluctance of his British allies that stopped him increasing direct American involvement during the struggle for Dien Bien Phu. In defiance of the Geneva agreements Eisenhower effectively made the United States the guarantor of an independent state of South Vietnam and committed the US to the defence of a particularly unpopular leader in Diem. He gave Diem billions of dollars worth of aid and 1,500 American advisers, nearly half of whom were military. Once such a commitment was undertaken, it was arguable that America had incurred an obligation to see it through. From that point it would prove to be but a short step to putting American soldiers into Vietnam.

In order to come to conclusions about Eisenhower's responsibility for the American involvement in Vietnam, several questions need to be answered. Could any American president be seen to ignore any 'threat' from Communism in the Cold War era? When one president had committed American foreign policy in a certain direction was it feasible for another to reverse it? Once America had greatly aided the anti-Communist side in South Vietnam could it legitimately then just dump them? Negative answers to any of those questions would seem to suggest that Eisenhower was right, and that what was right would inevitably lead to American involvement in Vietnam. However, much depends on the sort of questions one asks. Was Communism really such a threat to America? Was Vietnam going Communist really going to affect the course of the Cold War? Did America have any right to intervene in what was in effect an internal debate about what kind of government Vietnam should have? Negative answers to these questions would suggest Eisenhower was mistaken in his policies. On the other hand, many Americans agreed with him, raising final questions. Can any president transcend the prejudices and preoccupations of his time? And if he does, will he and his party get re-elected?

Summary Diagram
'Eisenhower and Two Vietnams'

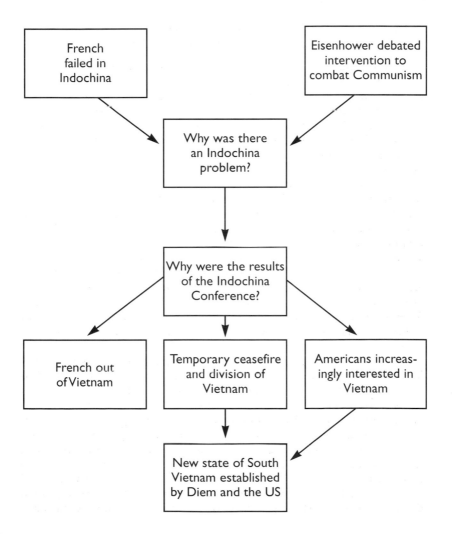

Your notes on Chapter 3 will need to be more detailed than those on Chapter 2. They should be geared primarily toward assessing the extent of Eisenhower's responsibility for US involvement in Vietnam and the wisdom of his decisions. You should also note any points which will illuminate why the Americans were later unable to defeat the Vietnamese Communists. A different approach would be to make notes on each major party's policies and actions, assessing their wisdom and success. This could be done in columns headed

DATES   USA   DIEM   VIETMINH   FRANCE   USSR   CHINA

Source-based questions often require you to 'contexturalise' sources, that is, to relate the sources to your background knowledge.

Specimen Question
Here is an example:
Look at the photos of Diem on page 29. Diem wanted both these photos widely publicised. Using these photos and your own knowledge, how successful would you say Diem was at public relations? (6 marks)

Specimen Answer
A good answer would assess these photos in the context of what is known about Diem's public relations, for example:
Diem aimed to appeal to traditional Vietnamese affections for the family and to Catholics by posing with his brothers, one a family man, the other an archbishop. Diem hoped the contemplative pose would make him appear statesmanlike and appealing to those Vietnamese who sought governmental stability. Diem's attempt to tap into these emotions constituted unsuccessful public relations in that the power he gave his family and Catholics was unpopular with the majority of Vietnamese. Similarly, Diem's aloof regality contrasted unfavourably with Ho's common touch. Good PR would have required the ability to listen to and understand others, to respond to requests for reform, and to relate to the ordinary people. Diem did none of those things. He disliked meeting ordinary people and had to be forced to do so by the Americans. His attempts at PR were unsuccessful.
Now attempt to answer the following set of questions on your own.

1. Eisenhower and a Communist Vietnam
Read Eisenhower and Joseph Alsop on Vietnam (page 22 and page 30).
a) In which part of Vietnam was the Mekong Delta? (1 mark)
b) Who were the Vietminh? (2 marks)

c) In what way do Eisenhower and Alsop seem to agree on the political system likely in a Communist-dominated Vietnam? In what way do they seem to disagree? (4 marks)

d) Using very brief quotations from the document, would you conclude that Alsop was pro- or anti-Communist? Why? (4 marks)

e) To what extent do you consider Alsop's description of life under the Vietminh to be accurate? (6 marks)

f) Using the two sources and your background knowledge, give reasons why Americans did not want a Communist Vietnam. (8 marks)

4 'Vietnam is the place' - the Kennedy Crusade (1961-3)

The last two chapters focused on what was happening in Vietnam and explained the US response to it. For Truman and Eisenhower Vietnam was a minor side-show in the Cold War. It was during the Kennedy presidency that Vietnam became far more important, although it was only under President Johnson that it became a national obsession.

There can be no doubt that the Kennedy presidency saw an increased commitment to South Vietnam: the facts and figures speak for themselves (see pages 43-4). However, since Kennedy's death there has been considerable debate over his policy. The debate has been affected by the knowledge that during the presidency of his successor the Vietnam war became highly controversial and unpopular. Kennedy supporters have been inclined to argue that the Vietnam war was 'Johnson's war' and that just before his assassination Kennedy was planning to get America out. Similarly, the Johnson administration was much criticised for its apparent lack of understanding of Vietnam and for reliance upon military solutions to the problems there. However, the study of the Kennedy administration's policies reveals similar failures of perception which are sometimes forgotten by those who concentrate upon Johnson's presidency in isolation.

There are thus several major issues for you to consider as you read this chapter. Why did Kennedy continue the American commitment to Vietnam? Would Kennedy have got out of Vietnam, had he lived? Was it Kennedy's (as opposed to Johnson's) war? Were Kennedy's Vietnam policies wise?

1 Kennedy's Early Ideas about Vietnam

By the time Kennedy became president in 1961 his ideas on Vietnam had already been shaped and demonstrated. Kennedy's Catholic family loathed Communism. The fanatically anti-Communist Senator Joseph McCarthy was a good friend of Kennedy's father and even dated Jack's sister. Like his party's leader President Truman, the young Democratic congressman Kennedy believed that the expansion of Communism must be 'contained' by America. Kennedy even attacked Truman for 'losing' China in 1949. Like most Americans, Kennedy believed in Eisenhower's domino theory, but he criticised that president for allowing the rise of Communism in the newly emergent nations of the Third World which Kennedy considered to be the new Cold War battleground. He criticised French colonialism in Indochina, believing that unless France granted independence to the people of Indochina, their thwarted nationalism might turn them to Communism and the remainder of Southeast Asia could well follow. After the 1954 Geneva agreements he believed that democracy could thrive in South Vietnam but rejected the idea of nation-wide elections, which he thought Ho would win. His fears of Third World Communism clearly outweighed his sympathy for nationalism and true democracy. In a 1956 speech to the American Friends of Vietnam he reiterated the domino theory, calling South Vietnam the

1   cornerstone of the free world in Southeast Asia, the keystone of the arch, the finger in the dike. Burma, Thailand, India, Japan, the Philippines, and obviously Laos and Cambodia ... would be threatened if the red tide of Communism overflowed in Vietnam ... [which was] a proving
5   ground for democracy in Asia ... [and] a test of American responsibility and determination in Asia ... [where] the relentless pressure of the Chinese Communists [must be stopped] ... No other challenge is more deserving of our effort and energy ... Our security may be lost piece by piece, country by country.

Kennedy criticised Eisenhower for losing the initiative in foreign policy and during his 1960 presidential election campaign Kennedy said that the country needed a president 'to get America moving again'. Militant anti-Communism was a keynote of his campaign rhetoric:

1   The enemy is the Communist system itself - implacable, insatiable, unceasing in its drive for world domination ... This is not a struggle for supremacy of arms alone. It is also a struggle for supremacy between two conflicting ideologies: freedom under God versus ruthless, godless
5   tyranny.

So, although most Americans were unaware of events in Vietnam when Kennedy became president (January 1961), his background suggested that he might be even more interested in and committed to Vietnam than his predecessors. This is why we must now shift our focus from Vietnam to Washington, DC.

2 The President and his Advisers

Once in power the interests, emphases and characters of Kennedy and his chosen advisers shaped US policy toward Vietnam.

a) President Kennedy - the Impatient Crusader

Kennedy's inaugural address was entirely devoted to foreign policy. It contained inspirational and now famous phrases:

> let every nation know, whether it wishes us well or ill, that we shall pay
> any price, bear any burden, meet any hardship, support any friend,
> oppose any foes to assure the survival and the success of liberty.

In some ways Kennedy was a prisoner of his own Cold War campaign
rhetoric - designed to win votes, it served to limit his foreign policy
options once in the White House. Having made much of the so-called
'missile gap' in 1960 and the need for a more dynamic foreign policy,
Kennedy was duty-bound to increase defence expenditure and
foreign involvement.

Kennedy was particularly sensitive about references to his youth
and inexperience and this made him keen to be assertive in foreign
affairs. An autumn 1961 White House luncheon was brought to a
horrified standstill when a newspaper editor challenged Kennedy:

> We can annihilate Russia and should make that clear to the Soviet
> government ... you and your Administration are weak sisters ...
> [America needs] a man on horseback ... Many people in Texas and the
> Southwest think that you are riding [your daughter] Caroline's tricycle.

A red-faced Kennedy who retorted 'I'm just as tough as you are' was
clearly a president who thought he had much to prove. He was well
aware that the nation was more likely to rally around a narrowly
elected president during a time of national crisis. His campaign
slogan had been 'a time for greatness' and he well knew that great
presidents are not easily made in tranquil times. In his book 'Profiles
of Courage' Kennedy had said that 'great crises make great men'.

Kennedy was convinced that the Third World was likely to be the
main future arena of the struggle between the US and the Soviet
Union. Khrushchev's rhetoric confirmed Kennedy's beliefs and fears,
for just before Kennedy's inauguration the Soviet leader had forecast
the ultimate triumph of Communism through wars of national liberation in Third World countries such as Vietnam, for which he
promised Soviet aid. Kennedy made the text of that speech compul-
sory reading for all in his administration, although ironically
Khrushchev's speech was not aimed at the US but at China, the
USSR's rival for the leadership of world Communism. The outgoing
President Eisenhower had warned Kennedy that the Republican Party
would attack 'any retreat in Southeast Asia', so if Kennedy was to
make a stand in the Third World it would probably be somewhere in
that region. The nature of that stand was likely to be shaped by
Kennedy's fascination with counter-insurgency (the use of guerrilla-
like tactics to counter Communist guerrillas in the Third World).
Kennedy's specially trained American counter-insurgency force wore
and became known as 'Green Berets'. Kennedy kept a green beret on
his Oval Office desk.

Kennedy's eagerness to get things moving made him impatient with
the State Department, so when he sought advice on foreign affairs he

looked to those in his close circle whom he trusted, such as Secretary of Defence Robert McNamara. Kennedy was thus influenced by the Defence Department rather than the State Department. The interests and emphases of the former were naturally very different from those of the professional diplomats of the latter. The Defence Department was naturally inclined to see problems in terms of military solutions. There was something about Kennedy's methods of seeking advice that made even his own brother, the Attorney-General Robert (Bobby) Kennedy, uneasy and critical:

1   The best minds in government should be utilised in finding solutions to … any problems. They should be available in times other than deep crises and emergencies as is now the case. You talk to McNamara but mostly on Defence matters, you talk to Dillon but primarily on financial
5   questions … These men should be sitting down and thinking of some of the problems facing us in a broader [con]text. I think you could get a good deal more out of what is available in Government than we are at the present time.

b) Secretary of Defence Robert McNamara - the Statistics Man

The son of a shoe salesman, McNamara attended two top American universities, Berkeley and Harvard. He taught accountancy at the Harvard Business School and the army utilised his statistical expertise in the Second World War. Medical bills for his wife's polio forced him to give up Harvard and seek greater financial rewards. He joined Henry Ford II's 'Whiz Kids' and had risen to the presidency of the Ford motor company when Kennedy offered him the Defence Department.

At Defence McNamara positively fizzed with energy. A colleague described him as a man who never walked but ran - even up escalators! The dynamic, tough-talking, fluent, competent and down-to-earth McNamara was the only cabinet member to become part of the charmed social circle around the president. Although McNamara was meticulous in his relations with Secretary of State Dean Rusk, taking care to give him due deference, McNamara's powerful personality coupled with Rusk's deliberately colourless public persona meant that his power within the cabinet was inevitably greater. Enormous influence and judgmental lapses on the part of McNamara proved unfortunate with regard to Vietnam. Like Rusk, McNamara was a great believer in the US commitment to Vietnam, but the Secretary of Defence's solutions to the problems in that faraway land were always military - an emphasis which proved unhelpful.

Behind his cool and rational exterior, McNamara was emotional and passionate in his beliefs. His good friend Bobby Kennedy thought him 'the most dangerous man in the Cabinet, because he is so persuasive and articulate'. A *New York Times* reporter commended his efficiency but found cause for concern in his total conviction of rectitude, his lack of historical knowledge and his tendency to try to reduce problems to statistics by eliminating the human factor. With regard to Vietnam, as McNamara subsequently admitted, these weaknesses were to prove disastrous. Trained in the importance of statistics, McNamara tended to look at numbers of weapons and men, while forgetting that poorly armed people will sometimes fight to the death for their independence. 'We were kidding ourselves into thinking that we were making well-informed decisions,' said one McNamara deputy years later.

c) Secretary of State Dean Rusk - the Quiet Professional

Born to a middle-class family which fell upon hard times, the poverty-stricken young Rusk was fascinated by politics and international relations. After spending three years at Oxford University on a scholarship, he returned to America and became a lecturer. Second World War desk service led him into the Truman State Department. Rusk believed that the appeasement of aggressors had led to the outbreak of war in Europe in 1939 and in the Pacific in 1941. His determination to oppose what he considered to be Communist aggression made him a hard-line Cold Warrior. He had had a considerable influence on America's Vietnam policy since the late 1940s.

While discussing choices for Secretary of State, Kennedy confessed that he wanted to dominate foreign policy personally, so the self-effacing Rusk seemed a good choice. After their first meeting Rusk told a friend 'Kennedy and I simply found it impossible to communicate. He didn't understand me and I didn't understand him.' Although in 1987 Rusk could not recall saying that, it seems to have been an accurate summary of their working relationship. Subsequently and frequently Rusk almost boasted that he had never been one of the 'in' crowd, saying with sarcastic undertones that he had never been pushed into Ethel Kennedy's swimming pool nor played touch football at the Kennedy compound in Hyannis Port. Bobby Kennedy particularly disliked him, claiming that Rusk had had a near mental and physical breakdown during the Cuban missiles crisis - a breakdown that appears to have escaped the notice of everyone else!

As Secretary of State, Rusk was irritated by the theatricality and amateurism of his boss, who listened to brother Bobby rather than the State Department experts. The president complained (to Rusk's underlings among others) that the methodical Rusk was frustrating, slow and indecisive. Rusk felt it his duty to put all the options before the president so that Kennedy could make an informed judgement. Kennedy preferred more decisive recommendations and scathingly referred to Rusk as 'a good errand boy'! Like McNamara, Rusk believed in American involvement in Vietnam, but as the fighting continued there, he felt it was the preserve of the Defence Department rather than the State Department. Unlike McNamara, Rusk never visited Vietnam, confirming the view that he saw it as a Defence Department operation.

Here then was an explosive situation. There was a crusading president keen to be assertive and to make a name for himself, who felt that the Third World and probably Southeast Asia was the next great Cold War arena; a president who listened to those more likely to put the emphasis on the military battles than upon the battles for the hearts and minds of the people. It is easy to see how all this would lead to increasing US military involvement in Vietnam.

3 Kennedy's Actions in the Third World

The ideas and characteristics of Kennedy and his advisers, as described above, help explain why the administration continued the American involvement in Vietnam and was likely to get involved militarily in the struggle against Communism in the Third World. We also need to look at what happened in Cuba and Laos to help us to understand why Kennedy not only continued but increased the American involvement in Vietnam.

a) Cuba - an Early Failure

In his first week in office Kennedy privately declared that the major problem areas of the Third World were the Congo, Cuba, Laos and Vietnam, the last being 'the worst we've got'. Despite a few warning voices within the administration, the US sponsored an unsuccessful landing in the Bay of Pigs in Communist Cuba in 1961. This Bay of Pigs fiasco bore many of the characteristics of the subsequent Vietnam experience. In Cuba, as in Vietnam, Kennedy felt bound to support an enterprise to which his predecessor had committed America and which took the form of military opposition to a popular nationalist leader who was also a Communist. Fidel Castro, like Ho, had a radical reform programme which many considered appropriate for a Third World country and he was by no means the inevitable tool of Moscow or Beijing. There was dissent within the Kennedy administration over Cuba as over Vietnam. Some talked of 'adventurism' in Cuba and said intervention would 'compromise our moral position in the world' but what social psychologists call 'group-think' (when the herd instinct halts independent thought or disagreement) proved triumphant. In both Cuba and Vietnam the Kennedy administration's policy and actions were neither systematically thought out, nor exhaustively discussed by all who might have contributed valuable ideas.

This Bay of Pigs failure naturally had an impact on US policy toward other Third World countries, including Laos.

b) Laos - Neither Winning Nor Losing

Of the three countries (Vietnam, Cambodia and Laos) that had emerged from French Indochina it was Laos that occupied Kennedy most in the early days of his presidency. Despite his friend's observation that Laos was not exactly 'a dagger pointed at the heart of Kansas' Kennedy feared a Soviet-backed Communist triumph there. In a March 1961 news conference he implied that the US might intervene militarily - an option favoured by the State Department, the CIA, the JCS, and his close advisers. However, as Bobby Kennedy subsequently recalled, President Kennedy was held back by the Bay of Pigs failure. Also, there were too few soldiers and aircraft available, and Congress feared intervention might lead to a Sino-American clash. Kennedy nevertheless sent US military advisers to assist the Laotian leader, an unpopular general whom he described as a 'total shit'. Then, between September 1961 and summer 1962, Kennedy's representative managed to 'neutralise' Laos: the superpowers agreed that it would be governed by a coalition. However, Laotian Communists proved unco-operative and Ho's Vietcong continued to use Laotian trails to get to South Vietnam, confirming Kennedy's feeling that the Communists must be stopped somewhere in Southeast Asia. Events in Laos thus contributed to the increased commitment to Vietnam, although it was not until the final year of Kennedy's presidency that Vietnam overtook Laos in his order of priorities.

c) How Cuba and Laos Helped Lead to Vietnam

The failure of the Bay of Pigs and the 'draw' consequent upon the supposed neutralisation of Laos meant that outright victories had to be won somewhere. The Bay of Pigs failure was countered by a 'triumphant' rejection of the option of an early privately negotiated solution to the Cuban missiles crisis, wherein a confrontational stance was preferred. Similarly, the backing down in Laos was countered by a firm commitment to Diem and South Vietnam. 'There are just so many concessions that one can make to the Communists in one year and survive politically,' Kennedy told a friend after the Bay of Pigs. 'We just can't have another defeat in Vietnam.' One insider has suggested that hawks within the administration would only accept neutrality in Laos in return for an activist policy in Vietnam.

Vietnam was 'better' than Laos in several ways. It had a long coastline where US naval supremacy could be brought to bear. Diem apparently had South Vietnam under control; and democracy seemed to have a good chance of working there. Given that the US was already committed to aid South Vietnam before Kennedy's presidency, and given that he had continued that commitment as president, a US departure would result in a loss of face and would 'undermine the credibility of American commitments everywhere' as Rusk and

McNamara told Kennedy. They pointed out that there would be 'bitter' divisions amongst the American public if Kennedy got out of Vietnam, and that 'extreme elements' would make political capital out of the retreat. Kennedy did not want to be accused of 'losing' Vietnam in the way that Truman had 'lost' China.

4 Kennedy and Diem

So far this chapter has concentrated upon the reasons why Kennedy continued and increased the American commitment to Vietnam. The remainder of this chapter looks at how the policies Kennedy actually pursued in Vietnam were made and the extent to which they were wise. This will illustrate further the extent of Kennedy's commitment to Vietnam, and also illuminate the debates over whether Vietnam was 'Kennedy's war' and whether or not he would have got America out of Vietnam, had he lived.

a) Military Solutions

It was not really until the summer of 1963 that Kennedy gave a great deal of attention to Vietnam. Until then he was preoccupied with other crises. Back in 1961 the journalist Stanley Karnow told the Kennedys that what he had seen in Vietnam was really ominous but Bobby was impatient: 'Vietnam, Vietnam ... we have thirty Vietnams a day here.' Dean Rusk and his State Department were more interested in the Soviet threat in Germany and seemed content to leave Vietnam to Robert McNamara's Defence Department. Tragically, that meant that Kennedy tended to see the Vietnam problem in terms of a military solution, especially as McNamara's team included several generals.

At Kennedy's accession, there were 800 American military advisers in South Vietnam. Within days of becoming president, Kennedy stepped up the financial aid to Diem to enable him to increase his army. The fact that Diem's quarter of a million soldiers could not wipe out roughly 12,000 Vietcong ought perhaps to have rung louder American alarm bells. The JCS and the National Security Council (NSC) recommended putting US ground troops in but Kennedy preferred to increase the number of advisers there. His Green Berets co-operated with the South Vietnamese army (ARVN) in counter-insurgency efforts. Diem's soldiers nevertheless continued to lose ground, so in October 1961 Kennedy sent Second World War hero General Maxwell Taylor to evaluate the military situation. The cultured Taylor was the president's favourite general and a great advocate of flexible response. Like Kennedy, Taylor felt that counter-insurgency would be effective against Communist guerrillas in the Third World. By this time there were over 2,000 American military advisers in Vietnam. Taylor recommended sending 8-10,000 American ground troops, while McNamara wanted to send 40,000 and even 200,000 if North Vietnam and China openly intervened.

The number of American military advisers rose alarmingly. There were 3,000 by December 1961 and 11,000 in 1962. Greater US aid included helicopters with American pilots used for transporting troops, reconnaissance and fire support. Although Kennedy publicly denied it, American pilot 'advisers' were actively involved in the war. Much of this was kept from the American public. In December 1961 the reporter Stanley Karnow saw a US aircraft carrier bringing 47 helicopters to Saigon. Shocked, he pointed the carrier out to a US officer who said, 'I don't see nothing.' More and more American advisers accompanied ARVN units on the ground. Kennedy authorised the use of napalm and defoliants which stripped the trees and enabled better aerial observation, but the military situation still deteriorated. The helicopters soon lost their shock value. Now the VC fired on them and could even bring them down. Disloyal and/or cowardly ARVN men deliberately used bombing to warn the VC away from certain areas. In January 1963 at Ap Bac 2,000 ARVN soldiers with American-operated helicopters, bombers, armoured personnel carriers and advisers refused to attack 350 lightly armed VC, resulting in the loss of five US helicopters and three pilots. The Americans had not helped in that they had delayed the attack by one day to enable American helicopter pilots to sleep off the excesses of New Year's Eve. Diem was unwilling to listen to American advice on the deployment of his troops: he feared losing too many men and preferred to use his best CIA-trained soldiers to keep himself in power. American officials estimated that Saigon controlled 49 per cent of the population, the VC 9 per cent, with the rest in dispute.

When McNamara visited Vietnam in 1962 he declared that 'every quantitative measurement we have shows we are winning the war', but this was a very dubious assertion. The military solution attempted by Kennedy and Diem was not working. There were many differing viewpoints within the Kennedy administration. Some wondered whether the solution was to send in American ground troops but Under-Secretary of State George Ball warned that 'we'll have three hundred thousand men in the paddies and jungles' within five years. 'George, you're crazier than hell,' said the president. 'That just isn't going to happen.' Kennedy sent a trusted liberal friend, Kenneth Galbraith, to Saigon to assess the situation. Galbraith criticised the administration's diagnosis that this was a military rather than a political problem and said Diem was a loser. Galbraith asked the president what difference there was between French colonialism and American activities in South Vietnam. Galbraith expressed incredulity that anyone in Kennedy's administration could claim that Vietnam was strategically important. He urged neutralisation, fearing that increased US involvement could only end in defeat and humiliation. In November 1962 Kennedy sent a leading Democratic senator to report on

Vietnam, but when the report was critical of Diem and the increasing American involvement Kennedy was displeased. Subsequent reports were a mixture of pessimistic references to Diem and the optimistic belief that American firepower must win eventually and that the VC could not afford to continue the struggle in the face of it. Rusk meanwhile warned that US involvement could provoke Hanoi and Beijing and destabilise Laos. When Kennedy visited France in May 1961, President de Gaulle had warned him:

> the more you become involved out there against Communism, the more the Communists will appear as the champions of national independence …You will sink step by step into a bottomless military and political quagmire, however much you spend in men and money.

These warnings and uncertainties made Kennedy cautious. He worried that American power might become over-extended. He felt that the Vietnamese situation was very complex, that this was not a clear-cut case of Communist aggression as Korea had been. He doubted that Congress and America's SEATO allies would be tempted to intervene in an obscure war so far away with so many guerrilla opponents, where millions had been spent for years without success. While he accepted that Diem needed a great deal more aid and advisers, Kennedy was as yet unwilling to send in US ground troops:

> The troops will march in, the bands will play; the crowds will cheer, and in four days everyone will have forgotten. Then we will be told we have to send in more troops. It's like taking a drink. The effect wears off, and you have to take another.

Were there alternatives to the military solution? In the contemporary Cold War climate, few dared suggest that the US should just get out, especially after one liberal who did so was virtually accused of Communism by Rusk. Kennedy sanctioned unofficial peace talks in the summer of 1962 but Hanoi's position was that America must get out before any meaningful negotiations could take place, so that was the end of that. One State Department expert suggested to Kennedy that it would be better to concentrate upon giving economic and social assistance to Vietnam. There were others in the State Department, the White House and Congress who felt the emphasis should not be on military solutions but on internal political, social and economic reform by Diem. It was however difficult to persuade Diem to reform.

b) The Reform Option

Kennedy was not convinced that Diem and the South Vietnamese really cared about the Cold War, democracy or freedom. Nevertheless in May 1961 he sent Vice-President Johnson to try to persuade Diem that one of the best ways to defeat the Communists was to introduce greater political, social and economic equality to South Vietnam.

Johnson urged Diem to reform and also tried flattery. On the advice of the State Department, Johnson proclaimed Diem to be another Churchill! Karnow asked Johnson if he really meant it. 'Diem's the only boy we got out there,' said Johnson. While recognising that Diem needed to introduce reforms, Johnson believed that it was a question of national honour to continue supporting 'friends' like Diem. Diem listened to the advice with conflicting emotions: nationalistic fears that Vietnam might become a US protectorate struggled with the realisation that his repressive regime was in trouble and that America might desert him altogether if he was too awkward.

From early 1962 America encouraged Diem to adopt the policy of 'strategic hamlets', fortified villages in which the Vietnamese peasants would hopefully be isolated from the Vietcong. Unfortunately the Vietcong frequently joined the other residents and played upon their discontent at being taken away from their ancestral lands and farms to build the stockades. The strategic hamlets scheme was run by Diem's brother Ngo Dinh Nhu who ignored US advice when establishing them, so that within a year the Vietcong captured thousands of US weapons from hamlets foolishly set up too far from Saigon. Karnow felt that Nhu was 'approaching madness' by this time. Concerned only with increasing his own power, Nhu ignored the social, economic and political reforms the US suggested he introduce in the hamlets, resulting in increased opposition to the Diem/US regime. Many years later it was revealed that Nhu's deputy in this business was a Communist who did his best to sabotage the scheme. The unpopular policies and personalities of Diem and his family and their reluctance to introduce reforms helped to ensure continued Communist successes.

c) The Most Important Woman in the Vietnam War

The Kennedy administration spent over two years helping the unpopular Diem, vainly trying to make him reform his government. Diem stubbornly persisted in repressive policies, relying upon his equally unpopular relations. One American diplomat likened Diem and his brother Nhu to Siamese twins, but Diem was not keen on Nhu's wife (nor indeed on any woman). However, Diem patiently suffered his formidable sister-in-law out of family loyalty.

Nhu had been his future mother-in-law's lover but in 1943 he had switched his attentions to the daughter whom he married. In the absence of any alternative candidate, she became the first lady of her bachelor brother-in-law, Diem, in 1955. Madame Nhu's family were very French in their outlook and her French-style low-necked dresses shocked some of the more old-fashioned Vietnamese. Although her first language was French and she could never write in Vietnamese, Madame Nhu made it clear that she considered herself to be like the patriotic and heroic sisters who had led the Vietnamese struggle against China in the first century AD. As first lady she promoted conservative legislation, including the banning of beauty contests, boxing matches and night-clubs. Cafés were allowed to remain open, provided that the prostitutes who frequented them wore white tunics like nurses! Many southern Vietnamese were traditionally tolerant in matters such as this and they developed an intense dislike of Madame Nhu and her decrees. When US Ambassador Lodge (see page 48) first met Diem he told him that many Americans thought Madame Nhu must be the leader of South Vietnam as they had seen her picture so often. In a rare moment of humour, Diem joked that he frequently threatened his sister-in-law that he would marry, thus depriving her of her supremacy.

Madame Nhu played an important role in the war in that her behaviour, policies and public statements (see page 48) helped make Diem even more unpopular in South Vietnam and in Washington.

d) The Debate Over Diem's Vietnam

During 1962 there was slowly increasing criticism of Diem's military and political ineptitude in the American press. This was led by Neil Sheehan of United Press International and David Halberstam of the *New York Times*. The latter was warned that he was on Diem's assassination list. Madame Nhu told reporters, 'Halberstam should be barbecued and I would be glad to supply the fluid and the match.' The Kennedy administration attempted to pressurise the *New York Times* into a change of viewpoint but failed, and then attacked the reporters as unpatriotic and tried to discredit them. Diem's police cornered several American reporters in a back alley in Saigon. They tried to kick one in the kidneys, retreating when the massive Halberstam charged, crying, 'Get back, get back, you sons of bitches, or I'll beat the shit out of you.' As yet the American press was not questioning the wisdom of involvement in Vietnam, just the tactics pursued and the results attained. Even so, Halberstam had a hard time persuading his editors to print what he wrote.

By the spring of 1963 relations between Diem and the US were very tense. Diem's refusal to work with the French had been a major cause of his rise to power, but it had become increasingly clear that he was incapable of working with anyone. Diem resented US 'advice' and seemed to be considering a settlement with Hanoi which would get the Americans out, while Kennedy told a journalist friend that,

> we don't have a prayer of staying in Vietnam ...These people hate us. They are going to throw our asses out ... But I can't give up a piece of territory like that to the Communists and then get the American people to re-elect me.

It is possible that their mutual Catholicism had played a part in Kennedy's support of Diem. However, Catholics were a minority in

South Vietnam and in spring 1963 there was trouble. The Diem regime allowed the flying of Catholic flags in honour of Diem's brother (an archbishop in the Catholic church) but banned flags for the celebration of Buddha's birthday. When 10,000 Buddhists protested Diem sent in soldiers. Seven Buddhists were killed. A 73-year-old Buddhist priest set himself alight in protest. His flesh burned away leaving only his heart which became an object of worship to the Buddhist majority. This dramatic protest made headlines in America. Other such deaths followed and Madame Nhu made things worse by flippant references to barbecued martyrs. 'Let them burn and we shall clap our hands,' she told the press. She and Diem remembered how hundreds of their ancestors had been murdered by Buddhists in the nineteenth century. Kennedy was shocked at the front page newspaper pictures of the Buddhist martyrs. 'How could this have happened?' he asked. 'Who are these people? Why didn't we know about them before?' If Kennedy really did not know of the Catholic-Buddhist tension, he had been lax in doing his homework on a country to which he had sent several thousand Americans. If he did know, he was indulging in one of his favourite tactics for deflecting blame from himself (he had blamed faulty intelligence for the Bay of Pigs fiasco).

By August Diem appeared to be waging religious war on the Buddhist majority, and the administration felt it was time for a new American ambassador. Ambassador Frederick Nolting, who knew little about Asia, was replaced by Henry Cabot Lodge II, who knew a little more.

e) Ambassador Lodge

A January 1963 State Department report had summarised America's problems in Vietnam:

1 There is no overall planning effort that effectively ties together the civilian and the military efforts. There is little or no long-range thinking about the kind of country that should come out of victory and about what we do now to contribute to this longer-range goal...The real
5 trouble, however, is that the rather large US effort in South Vietnam is managed by a multitude of independent US agencies and people with little or no overall direction. No one man is in charge...What is needed, ideally, is to give authority to a single, strong executive, a man perhaps with a military background but who understands that this war is essen-
10 tially a struggle to build a nation out of the chaos of revolution. One possibility would be to appoint the right kind of general as Ambassador. An alternative would be to appoint a civilian public figure whose character and reputation would permit him to dominate the representatives of all the other departments and agencies.

The State Department clearly felt the need for a new ambassador to Vietnam. Was Lodge the right man for the job? In some ways he was.

Lodge was a patriot, Second World War military hero, and an experienced and ambitious Republican politician with a particular interest in foreign affairs. When Kennedy offered the post to Lodge he was worried about the photos of the burning monks and said that one of Lodge's main tasks would be to improve relations with the American press, sections of which were attacking US support of Diem. From this point of view Kennedy had chosen the right man, for Lodge's relations with the press were good and he was well aware of its importance. Talking of the Diem regime in August 1963, Lodge said,

> The United States can get along with corrupt dictators who manage to stay out of the newspapers. But an inefficient Hitlerism, the leaders of which make fantastic statements to the press, is the hardest thing on earth for the US Government to support.

On the other hand, as Nolting said, Lodge was simply 'a piece of Republican asbestos to keep the heat off Kennedy'. Some of those close to Kennedy were shocked at the appointment, knowing Kennedy's low opinion of Lodge's political talents. As so often with Kennedy, personal feelings played a role in his policies: one White House insider said the president was keen to deflate a pompous old rival and therefore approved the appointment 'because the idea of getting Lodge mixed up in such a hopeless mess as Vietnam was irresistible'. Lodge was not ideal for the co-ordinating role envisaged by the State Department. He lacked practice in team work and administration. In some ways he was like Kennedy himself, preferring to use his own sources of information rather than utilise the collective wisdom of all the American agencies in Vietnam.

Rusk told Lodge in June 1963 that Vietnam had become a great burden to the president. It was now taking up more of the president's time than any other issue. Rusk sent Lodge on his way with the comment that,

> we need an ambassador out there who is tough; who can act as a catalyst; who will take responsibility and make decisions and not refer many detailed questions to Washington. We want to make the political side of things go as well as the military side has been going.

Lodge was indeed 'tough' and he certainly did 'act as a catalyst'.

f) Washington, Lodge and the Plotters

Lodge believed that 'our help to the [South Vietnamese] regime in past years inescapably gives us a responsibility that we cannot avoid', and that victory was impossible if Diem remained in power. Once in Vietnam, Lodge was encouraged to learn of an ARVN plot against Nhu. An anti-Diem group in the Kennedy administration got a preoccupied president to agree that Diem must be got rid of unless he instituted dramatic changes, especially with regard to Nhu and his wife.

There had been no real discussion about this, to the anger of McNamara and other influential men. Kennedy had been relaxing on Cape Cod and absorbed by the forthcoming civil rights march on Washington. One member of the administration said that the whole confused episode taught them 'never do business on the weekend.' The administration grew ever more divided over the Diem issue. 'My God,' said the president, 'my government's coming apart.' On 31 August 1963 an NSC meeting reviewed the prospects of working with Diem. A State Department expert on Vietnam was unimpressed by those present - Rusk, McNamara, Maxwell Taylor, Johnson and Bobby Kennedy:

> 1   I listened for about an hour or an hour and a half, before I was asked to say anything at the meeting and they looked to me absolutely hopeless, the whole group of them. There was not a single person there who knew what he was talking about. They were all great men. It was
> 5   appalling to watch. They did not know Vietnam. They did not know the past. They had forgotten the history. They simply did not understand the identification of nationalism and Communism, and the more this meeting went on, the more I sat there and I thought, 'God, we're walking into a major disaster.'

The State Department expert gave the others his opinions on Vietnam but they dismissed them.

Meanwhile, in the absence of firm leadership from Washington, Ambassador Lodge acquired an unusual amount of control of US policy in Vietnam. In his first meeting with Diem, aware of Diem's interview tactics, Lodge took the initiative and began to criticise Madame Nhu. Lodge then made the common mistake of letting Diem talk, which Diem did without pause for two hours. Lodge could not get another word in and therefore decided to try to avoid further encounters. He proceeded to turn Congress and American public opinion against Diem and Nhu, through press 'leaks' on their activities and by establishing highly publicised shelters for persecuted Buddhists in the US embassy. Meanwhile, the ARVN plotters were unconvinced of total US support and they began to falter while the Washington search for a meaningful policy continued. Kennedy's disunited administration rejected both the option of using US combat troops and the idea of a total withdrawal. In a September interview Kennedy criticised the Saigon regime and said:

> we can help them, we can give them equipment, we can send our men ... as advisers, but they have to win it - the people of Vietnam - against the Communists.

He acknowledged that Diem needed to change his policies and personnel. In another interview three days later Kennedy reiterated the domino theory and warned of the influence of expansionist China in Vietnam.

Kennedy sent two more observers to Vietnam. The Defence Department representative concentrated upon US military activity and was optimistic, the State Department representative concentrated upon the Diem regime and was pessimistic. 'You two did visit the same country, didn't you?' queried the exasperated president. 'This is impossible. We can't run a policy when there are such divergent views on the same set of facts.' Kennedy then sent McNamara and the Chairman of the JCS, General Maxwell Taylor, to report. Their itinerary was dictated by the military in Vietnam and this, coupled with their own unwillingness to admit their earlier optimism had been unjustified, led them to say that all was going well militarily and that the 16,000 US forces could be withdrawn by 1965. Kennedy announced that 1,000 would leave in late 1963 but omitted to mention that others would replace them! Encouraged by Lodge, McNamara and Taylor had been critical of Diem. By this time Nhu was negotiating with Hanoi, confirming the American conviction that he and Diem had to go. Bobby Kennedy floated the idea that perhaps 'now was the time to get out of Vietnam entirely' but there was no one in the administration willing to take up the challenge to look at the problem afresh.

The ARVN plotters now knew that they would have America's tacit support in their coup. The White House said it did not wish to 'stimulate' a coup but that it would not 'thwart' one and would help any new regime. The debate about the wisdom of dumping Diem continued until the coup occurred. Lodge had given vital encouragement but publicly he denied any US involvement. It was perhaps naive to think there could be a coup but no assassinations. 'Every Vietnamese has a grin on his face today,' said Lodge triumphantly but Kennedy heard the news of the assassination of Diem and Nhu 'with a look of shock and dismay'. During 1970s investigations of CIA complicity in plots to assassinate Castro, Kennedy's speech writer said the idea of assassination was 'totally foreign' to Kennedy's 'reverence for human life and his respect for his adversaries' and his 'insistence upon a moral dimension in US foreign policy'. In November 1961 Kennedy himself had told the *New York Times* that 'morally' the US must not be a party to assassination. 'If we get into that kind of thing, we'll all be targets.' We might never know for certain whether Kennedy tacitly approved the idea of assassinating his Cuban enemy Castro or his Vietnamese friend Diem, but it seems possible that he did. Ironically Kennedy himself would meet the same fate as Diem within three weeks. 'The chickens have come home to roost,' said Madame Nhu with grim satisfaction.

At the moment of Kennedy's death there were 23,000 American 'advisers' in Vietnam.

5 Assessment

What would Kennedy have done next had he lived? He was talking of a thorough review of America's Vietnam policy just before he died. Some of his intimates insist he would have got America out of Vietnam. Kennedy told one senator friend 'I can't [get out] until 1965 - after I'm re-elected.' However, Rusk, Johnson and Bobby Kennedy were among those who said he had no plans to get out. Indeed, Bobby, who knew him best, said that in effect his brother had no plans at all! One biographer describes Kennedy's Vietnam policy as a shambles at the time of his death. The formulation of that policy raises many questions about the leadership qualities of John Fitzgerald Kennedy, and about the way he selected and listened to advisers. It also raises disturbing questions about the difficulties of conducting foreign policy in a democracy (see page 33).

Kennedy's perception of the importance of little Vietnam seems ludicrous to us, but it must be said that in the contemporary Cold War context many other Americans agreed with him. Early setbacks in his presidency (the Bay of Pigs and the Vienna summit with Khrushchev) caused Kennedy to confide to a *New York Times* reporter, 'Now we have a problem in making our power credible, and Vietnam is the place.' Particular events confirmed and shaped Kennedy's Cold War mentality, leading him into increased commitment to Vietnam. That country's internal politics and Diem's failings in particular led to confusion for, having decided that 'Vietnam is the place' and having continued the commitment to Diem, it was then difficult for Kennedy to admit that this was all a mistake. Getting rid of Diem did not improve the situation and served to confirm the tendency to believe that in the absence of any other constructive ideas, increased force would somehow do the trick. General Westmoreland subsequently attributed enormous significance to the American role in the demise of Diem. It 'morally locked us in Vietnam'. By encouraging a change of government in South Vietnam, Kennedy greatly increased America's obligation to subsequent Saigon governments.

Following the route sketched out by his predecessors, Kennedy had interpreted events in Vietnam within a Cold War context which did not really apply. Ho Chi Minh was neither a Moscow nor a Beijing puppet and it could be argued that Kennedy had invested Vietnam with a Cold War importance that it did not really merit. Despite his frequent uncertainty about the wisdom of US involvement, he had increased his country's commitment to an unpopular regime which he then helped to overthrow in the last weeks of his life. The Kennedy administration claimed to be promoting democracy in South Vietnam but had supported a dictator and then a military clique. The nature of that US support was primarily military and financial and the reforming efforts of the non-military American personnel were handicapped by the unpleasant nature of the South Vietnamese regimes. Kennedy had passed a poisoned chalice to his successor.

Summary Diagram
'"Vietnam is the Place" - the Kennedy Crusade (1961-3)'

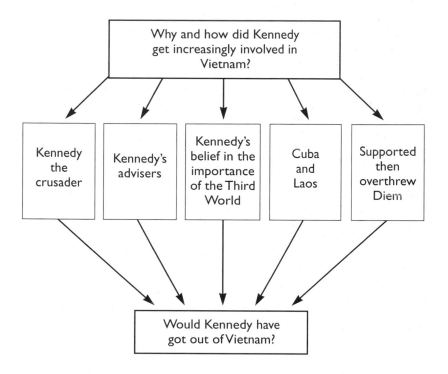

Making notes on '"Vietnam is the place" - the Kennedy Crusade'

You should make detailed notes on this chapter, concentrating on why Kennedy continued and increased the American commitment to Vietnam, and assessing the wisdom of his policy. It would be useful to recap Chapters 2 and 3, making notes summarising why, how and how far America was involved during the presidencies of Truman, Eisenhower and Kennedy, picking out possible turning-points when the commitment became irreversible, giving reasons to justify your choices.

Answering essay questions on '"Vietnam is the place" - the Kennedy Crusade'

Examiners favour certain themes in their questions on Kennedy and Vietnam:

1. How and why did he increase US involvement?
2. Was his policy successful?
3. Was his policy wise?

There are two styles of essay question. One type is structured for you, effectively giving you sub-headings to guide you through your essay. The other kind simply gives you one question or debate and expects you to answer at length without further assistance from the examiner. The above questions on Kennedy would probably be of the latter kind. If you would prefer to consider a structured question first, look at page 110 and then come back to this one when you revise.

Question 1 requires you to trace the stages by which Kennedy got more involved (i.e. 'how') and to explain his motives at each stage (i.e. 'why'). Questions like this can be answered using a chronological approach, but do not forget that while chronological essays DECREASE organisational problems they INCREASE the likelihood of an answer which is weighted far more toward narrative than analysis, instead of containing a balance between the two. One way in which to ensure that a chronologically organised essay contains sufficient analysis is by beginning and/or ending every paragraph with some points about the WHY which are appropriate to the chronological account at that point.

Questions 2 and 3 do not lend themselves to a chronological approach. Answers which have to give an assessment of success/failure or wise/unwise are probably best begun with a definition. Introductory paragraphs are particularly important here, as the examiner will want to know how you judge success before you begin to make claims one way or the other.

Specimen Introduction

After reading this suggested introduction for Question 2 (see below) you might like to try an introduction for Question 3.

A possible introduction to the essay question, 'Was Kennedy's Vietnam policy a success?'

Early in his presidency, Kennedy said Vietnam was one of the greatest problems facing America. Subscribing to the containment and domino theories, Kennedy was sure that the loss of Vietnam to Communism would have a knock-on effect in other Southeast Asian countries. Believing that the American democracy was more secure in a world without Communism and that democracy was intrinsically desirable, he felt that America should support the South Vietnamese opponents of Communism. Thus by his own standards Kennedy's Vietnam policy would be 'successful' if he stopped South Vietnam from falling to Communism. It is true that at his death the South Vietnamese government remained anti-Communist, but the stability of that government was doubtful. By late 1963 America had effectively replaced the authoritarian government of Diem with a small military clique - an even more undemocratic government, propped up by the world's leading democracy. Neither Kennedy nor the increasingly critical American press claimed that America's Vietnam policy was successful, for while few Americans would have been happy to see another country become Communist, the survival of a democratic and independent South Vietnam seemed uncertain.

That introduction tries to establish what Kennedy would have considered to have been a successful policy. It then suggests that he had failed by his own standards - and by those of some other Americans. The last few lines indicate to the examiner that the remainder of the essay is going to look at his policies and see how and why they failed to ensure the survival of South Vietnam. It is helpful to have some factual content in an introduction, otherwise it can seem very vague. In essays where you are asked to consider success or failure, some 'before and after' facts are helpful - in this example, the nature of the South Vietnamese government is described so that one can see the situation there was deteriorating, indicating a Kennedy failure.

Source-based questions on '"Vietnam is the place" - the Kennedy Crusade'

Source-based questions often ask you to compare the evidence presented in several sources, asking if and how they differ. An example of this is given below.

Specimen Question
Look at the comments of de Gaulle on page 45 and the State Department report on page 48. How do they differ in their views of the likelihood of American success in Vietnam? [4 marks]

Specimen Answer
Your answer might go like this:
De Gaulle sees American involvement in Vietnam as doomed to defeat, as foreigners inevitably make Communists 'appear as the champions of national independence'. The State Department does not see Vietnamese nationalism as the problem. They feel that all America needs is 'one [American] man in charge' of the political and military efforts in South Vietnam, while de Gaulle has learned from France's experience that no amount of foreign effort is effective

against Vietnamese nationalism. The Americans fail to see that if they have to run South Vietnam for the South Vietnamese, then South Vietnam is not a viable state. [The best answers to comparison questions usually avoid dealing with one source first then the other, instead combining comments about the two together.]

Attempt to answer the following questions on your own.

1. Kennedy's Speeches (in 1956 and 1961)

Look at Kennedy's speeches in 1956 (page 37) and 1961 (page 38) and 1963 (page 50). Answer the following questions.

a) To which popularly accepted principle is Kennedy subscribing when he talks of other countries being threatened if Vietnam fell to Communism? In whose administration did this principle become popular? (2 marks)

b) What did Kennedy mean by 'the relentless pressure of the Chinese Communists'? (2 marks)

c) In what ways does the third speech seem to differ from the other two? Refer to both content and tone in your answer. (6 marks)

d) What are the strengths and weaknesses of these sources for a historian considering whether or not Kennedy would have got America out of Vietnam had he lived? (7 marks)

e) Using these sources and your background knowledge, discuss whether Kennedy would or would not have got America out. (8 marks)

5 'Johnson's War'?

1 Introduction

President Johnson's real preoccupation was social reform - he wanted a 'Great Society'. Yet he sent nearly a million American soldiers to Vietnam and became the president most associated with and hated for what he called 'that bitch of a war'.

In this chapter we will look at what is probably the major question facing anyone studying American involvement in Vietnam. Was it Johnson's war? In order to decide one has to investigate why and how he continued and escalated the involvement, examining at every stage the extent to which others shared responsibility.

2 Why Johnson Continued the War

Given the American world-view in 1963, the circumstances of Johnson's accession to the presidency, and the presidential advisers, Johnson's continuation of the war seems almost inevitable.

a) A Man of his Time

Johnson aroused much hostile criticism for 'his' war, but he was just like many other Americans of his time in his patriotism, anti-Communism and misunderstanding of foreigners.

Johnson was intensely patriotic. In 1966 he told some soldiers that his great-great-grandfather had died in the heroic struggle against Mexico at the Alamo in 1836. The fact that this was untrue is a clear indication of Johnson's tremendous pride in national tradition and the military. In the Senate he always voted to build up the armed forces. America had always been victorious in wars. Defeat by what he called 'that damn little pissant country', 'that raggedy-ass little fourth-rate' Vietnam was inconceivable.

Like many Americans, Johnson genuinely believed his country fought for world freedom as well as American security in two world wars, in Korea and in Vietnam. Like many of his generation, he abhorred the idea of appeasing an enemy: 'If you let a bully come into your front yard one day, the next day he'll be up on your porch, and the day after that he'll rape your wife in your own bed.' As vice-president, Johnson firmly believed that America should fight Communist 'aggressors' in Southeast Asia whatever the cost. Like Kennedy and Eisenhower, Johnson believed Vietnam was a 'domino': if it fell to Communism the countries around it would rapidly follow suit. He felt that America had a debt of honour. His country had to continue to help South Vietnam because of US membership of SEATO (see page 27). America had to be seen to be standing by her allies.

Like many Americans, Johnson found it quite difficult to under-stand foreign affairs and foreigners. 'The trouble with foreigners is that they're not like the folks you were reared with,' he said. Johnson read and travelled widely but it did not necessarily lead to greater understanding. On a vice-presidential visit to Thailand he was furious when a fellow American advised him against shaking hands with the Thais, who dislike physical contact with strangers. 'Damn it,' cried Johnson, 'I have shaken hands with people everywhere and they have all loved it!' He felt Ho Chi Minh was another Hitler and should be treated accordingly.

Did Johnson's patriotism, anti-Communism and misunderstanding of foreigners make it inevitable that he would continue American involvement in Vietnam? Perhaps not. He knew that a long war would probably lose the support of Congress and the public. He knew the weaknesses of the Saigon government. In 1961 he said Diem must reform and fight his own war. He knew that only China and the USSR would benefit if America got 'bogged down chasing guerrillas' over Asiatic rice fields and jungles. Nevertheless, he continued the American involvement. One major reason was the Kennedy legacy.

b) The Impact of Kennedy's Assassination on Johnson's Vietnam Policy

Johnson fretted at the insignificance of vice-presidential tasks. During his vice-presidency it would have crossed his mind that Kennedy's death was all that stood between him and the world's greatest office. He resented the younger and less experienced man being president. Amidst the sorrow Johnson felt at Kennedy's death there was also joy at attaining the presidency. Guilt feelings contributed to his determin-ation to stand by all Kennedy had done and those who had helped Kennedy do it. 'I swore to myself that I would carry on,' Johnson subsequently explained. 'I would continue for my partner who had gone down ahead of me ... When I took over, I often felt as if President Kennedy were sitting there in the room looking at me.' Two days after Kennedy's assassination, the new president told Ambassador Lodge he was not going to 'lose Vietnam ... Tell those generals in Saigon that Lyndon Johnson intends to stand by our word.' 'My first major decision on Vietnam had been to reaffirm President Kennedy's policies,' Johnson said later. The tragic circum-stances of Johnson's accession to power thus caused him to make a vital decision with little apparent debate and discussion. Emotionally and constitutionally, the new president felt he had to continue the policies of his properly elected predecessor.

There is a case for calling Vietnam 'Kennedy's war'. Kennedy had increased American involvement in Vietnam. As vice-president, Johnson had opposed American support for the coup against Diem, realising that it dramatically increased American obligation to subsequent Saigon regimes. However, Kennedy's death ensured that Johnson would not repudiate his predecessor's Vietnam policy. Knowing he had no real popular mandate, the new president hesitated to abandon any Kennedy commitment or Kennedy officials. The retention of Kennedy's advisers helped to ensure continued involvement in Vietnam.

c) Johnson and his Advisers

In order to decide whether Vietnam was 'Johnson's war', his relationship with his advisers must be investigated. Did they share responsibility for the war? Johnson thought he was the boss. He told his advisers he wanted a 'kiss-my-ass-at-high-noon-in-Macy's-window and tell me it smells like roses' loyalty. He wanted every assistant's 'pecker in my pocket'. He made his aides work with him while he defecated in the bathroom. Johnson said he wanted honesty, good judgement, and sound ideas from advisers but, understandably, they often just said what he wanted to hear. In 1966 an official told Stanley Karnow that Johnson's friend Judge Abe Fortas was his most influential adviser on Vietnam. 'But Fortas doesn't know anything about Vietnam,' exclaimed Karnow. 'True,' said the official, 'but he knows a lot about Lyndon Johnson.' Some think Johnson had a closed mind, but others say he was poorly advised on Vietnam.

Johnson's freedom of action and thought were inevitably circumscribed. In the circumstances of his accession to power he was tied to Kennedy's men. Johnson's retention of Kennedy men such as McNamara and Rusk meant that no fresh ideas emerged on the Vietnam problem. Rusk was obsessive about continuing the struggle in Southeast Asia. He believed withdrawal would cause loss of faith in America's commitment to oppose Communist aggression and lead to World War Three. McNamara was so important in making policy that some called Vietnam 'McNamara's war'. In his memoirs (1995) McNamara criticises both himself and Johnson's other civilian and military advisers for an inability to ask the searching and relevant questions that needed to be asked at every stage of US involvement in Vietnam. McNamara laments the administration's lack of historical knowledge and understanding of matters such as Sino-Vietnamese rivalry (there was a scarcity of China experts in the State Department due to the McCarthy hysteria).

There were some warning voices. In 1963 the influential Democratic Senate majority leader, Mike Mansfield, suggested a united and neutralised Vietnam. Johnson rejected this, correctly predicting that it would soon lead to the swift communisation of the whole of Vietnam. Johnson, Rusk and McNamara assured Mansfield that if the South Vietnamese government adopted political, economic and social policies to win over their people there would be no need for major and direct US involvement. Mansfield knew that the Saigon government was unlikely to reform. He never gave up. He kept asking Johnson pertinent questions:

- Why should a democracy like the US support military governments in Saigon?
- Did the people of South Vietnam really want a crusade against Communism?
- What US interest was a stake in little Vietnam?

Johnson did not want this kind of discussion. 'The president expects that all senior officers of the government will move energetically to insure the full unity of support for ... US policy in Vietnam,' said a secret memorandum of November 1963. Although the CIA was gloomy about the situation in Vietnam, many in the administration believed America would somehow triumph. The Kennedy men remaining in the State and Defence Departments and the White House wanted to save face. No one wanted to admit past errors. No one seemed to want real debate.

In wartime the beliefs and advice of the military were inevitably influential. Like Kennedy, Johnson found some military men scary, especially Air Force chief Curtis LeMay. LeMay wanted to 'bomb Vietnam back into the Stone Age'. However, Johnson inherited involvement in a war and as commander-in-chief felt duty-bound to listen to the generals. As Vietnam was the only war the generals had, they wanted to continue with it and indeed escalate it in order to win. Johnson's personal political ambition reinforced what the generals were advising. He repeatedly said he did not want to be the first president to lose a war, especially to the Communists. Johnson's military and civilian advisers and his own beliefs and ambitions thus guided him toward the continuation of the commitment to Vietnam, even though the situation there was deteriorating.

d) Early Debates and Decisions

From December 1963 Hanoi sent increasing numbers of North Vietnamese Army (NVA) regulars south, which greatly strengthened the VC. Diem's successor retreated to his tennis court and his garden where he raised orchids. He was soon deposed. His successors were equally unimpressive. The strategic hamlets programme was clearly a failure and the VC impressively countered US air power with ever-increasing supplies of Soviet and Chinese weaponry. It was estimated that the Communists controlled around half of South Vietnam. General Maxwell Taylor and McNamara visited Saigon and in March 1964 described the situation as 'very disturbing'. The South Vietnamese were generally apathetic and unwilling to fight. Taylor, McNamara and the JCS favoured direct action against North Vietnam. LeMay said North Vietnam should be bombed because 'we are swatting flies [in South Vietnam] when we should be going after the manure pile [North Vietnam]'. Johnson felt the war needed to be won quickly before Congress demanded American withdrawal. Early in the Johnson presidency Vietnam was supposedly being 'reassessed' every day, but what was being reassessed by the Johnson administration was not WHETHER American involvement should continue but HOW it should continue.

On 20 April 1964, Johnson publicly declared that America was 'in this battle as long as South Vietnam wants our support' in its fight for freedom, but his private doubts were revealed in a May 1964 conversation:

1 I don't think the people of the country know much about Vietnam, and I think they care a hell of a lot less. We tell [Moscow, Beijing and Hanoi] ... that we'll get out of there [Vietnam] ... if they will just quit raiding their neighbours. And they say 'Screw you'. All the senators are all
5 saying 'Let's move, let's go into the North.' They'd impeach a president that would run out, wouldn't they? ... I stayed awake last night thinking of this thing ... It looks to me like we're getting into another Korea ... I don't think that we can fight them ten thousand miles away from home ... I don't think it's worth fighting for. And I don't think that we can get
10 out. It's just the biggest damned mess ... What the hell is Vietnam worth to me? ... What is it worth to this country? ... Of course if you start running from the Communists, they may just chase you into your own kitchen ... This is a terrible thing we're getting ready to do.

3 How Johnson Was Able to Escalate the War

By July 1964 200 Americans had died in Vietnam, and Johnson had added 2,500 men to the US forces there. South Vietnam's war against the Communists was not going well but debate in Washington centred on how to help Saigon win it, not how to get out of it. Most of Johnson's advisers, led by Rusk and McNamara, now urged escalation. If it were necessary for success, they argued, America should even strike at North Vietnam itself.

Johnson thought that if the time came for escalation of American involvement in Vietnam, he would need congressional and public support. He believed that he obtained the former with the Gulf of Tonkin resolution, and the latter in the presidential election of November 1964.

a) August 1964 - The Gulf of Tonkin Resolution

For a decade the CIA had been secretly sending South Vietnamese teams on sabotage missions to the North. In the first half of 1964 South Vietnamese gunboats raided North Vietnam's coast and Johnson approved covert American operations. American ships such as the 'Maddox' went on espionage missions in the North's coastal waters.

During the summer of 1964, the Republican presidential candidate

Barry Goldwater was accusing Johnson of being 'soft on Communism', so the president wanted to appear firm. Johnson claimed that the North Vietnamese made two unprovoked attacks on the 'Maddox' in the Gulf of Tonkin. On 4 August 1964 he asked for congressional support for avenging the attacks. The administration introduced a resolution originally designed in June to raise Saigon's morale. The Gulf of Tonkin incident gave Johnson the opportunity to get this resolution passed. Believing that the lives of innocent American sailors had been jeopardised by the North Vietnamese, Congress willingly passed the Gulf of Tonkin resolution. The resolution gave the president the power to wage war in Vietnam: as Johnson said, it was 'like grandma's night-shirt - it covered everything'. In its final form the resolution said North Vietnamese naval units,

1   in violation of international law, have deliberately and repeatedly attacked United States naval vessels lawfully present in international waters ... The United States regards as vital to its national interest and to world peace the maintenance of international peace and security in
5   Southeast Asia. Consonant [in accordance] with the Constitution of the United States and the Charter of the United Nations and in accordance with its obligations under the Southeast Asia Collective Defence Treaty, the United States is, therefore, prepared, as the President determines, to take all necessary steps, including the use of armed force, to assist
10 any member or protocol state of the Southeast Asia Collective Defence Treaty requesting assistance in defence of its freedom.

The resolution would expire when the president believed the situation in Southeast Asia was safe or when Congress decided to terminate it. A few senators led by Mansfield were unconvinced that America was acting correctly. One bitterly pointed out that they had no choice but to support the president when he said there was a crisis. Another said 'all Vietnam is not worth the life of a single American boy' but no one listened. The Senate had been two-thirds empty for the debate on the resolution, which it passed 88 to 2.

Should Congress be blamed for giving Johnson the power to escalate the war? Johnson and McNamara were not totally open with them about the covert raids, the incident or the implementation of the resolution. Did the administration wait for and even create the incident in order to get the resolution passed? The American naval missions were provocative and there are many doubts surrounding the second North Vietnamese 'attack'. 'Hell,' the president admitted years later, 'for all I know, our navy was shooting at whales out there.' Did Johnson exploit events both to escalate US military involvement in Vietnam and to win over the American public in an election year? While Johnson was trying to decide whether there had been a second attack, the press reported the supposed incident and Johnson felt trapped, fearing that if he did nothing his Republican opponent in the presidential election would call him a coward. The results and significance of the passage of the resolution were great. With the resolution, Johnson appeared to have the nation behind him. Now the war could really be taken to the North: American aircraft bombed North Vietnam for the first time. This escalation made Johnson look tough. His public approval rating rose from 42 per cent to 72 per cent, helping him win the presidential election. Ominously, American prestige was even more firmly committed to defending South Vietnam. Should another escalatory step seem necessary it would be even easier. The resolution and the presidential election suggested a nation united behind its president in his Vietnam policy.

b) The 1964 Presidential Election

During the election campaign the administration became aware that the voters were asking many questions about Vietnam:

- Why are we still there?
- Why are we there at all?
- Why haven't we trained the Vietnamese to do their own fighting?
- Why can't we win?
- Why can't it be a UN effort like Korea?
- Would it be so disastrous if we got out?

Foreign policy issues are rarely decisive in American presidential elections but they were probably more important than usual in 1964. The Republican candidate Barry Goldwater was prone to verbal gaffes. When he said that America ought to use all her strength to win in Vietnam, he was seen as a trigger-happy hawk. He was widely if wrongly perceived as recommending the use of atomic weapons on Hanoi, while Johnson was perceived as the peace candidate. Goldwater said that as Vietnam was 'a national burden' and the people were divided over both the legitimacy of US involvement and the conduct of the war, it was not in America's best interests to make the war a campaign issue. Johnson was greatly relieved. This meant there was no great open debate on Vietnam. Johnson knew that if left-wingers accused him of being a war-monger or if right-wingers accused him of being 'soft on Communism' he might not get re-elected. He therefore reassured the left by saying he did not intend to do anything rash or have a major war. He made a promise that might have been crucial to his re-election: 'We are not going to send American boys away from home to do what Asian boys ought to be doing for themselves.' On the other hand, he reassured the right by saying 'America keeps her word.' At Christmas 1963 he had told the JCS he did not want to lose South Vietnam OR get America into a war before the election: 'Just let me get elected and then you can have your war.' He also gained votes by appearing tough over the Gulf of Tonkin incident.

Did Johnson plan to escalate once elected? Like Kennedy, Johnson hoped that Saigon would be able to win its own war. During the election campaign neither he nor his advisers knew for sure exactly what to do about Vietnam, but most were reluctantly concluding that escalation was the only answer. He concentrated first on winning the election. Having won, he believed he had a popular mandate to do as he saw fit.

4 Why Did Johnson Escalate?

The Gulf of Tonkin resolution and Johnson's election as president help explain how he was able to escalate. We now have to investigate why he escalated. Again we will see that he had plenty of support, that this was not just 'Johnson's war'.

Some people believe that Johnson's combative personality made escalation inevitable. Some make much of his macho Texas background, suggesting that such an aggressive man would seek military solutions to problems. Many consider him over-confident. Johnson was often arrogant. When finally elected president in his own right in November 1964 he said, 'I've been kissing asses all my life and I don't have to kiss them any more. Tell those press bastards of yours that I'll see them when I want to and not before.' That kind of arrogance perhaps led on some occasions to an uncritical belief in his own rectitude. However, generalisations about Johnson's character are probably unhelpful. Sometimes there was fear and uncertainty behind his confident bluster. Privately and frequently he admitted that he did not know what to do about Vietnam. More often than not, he responded to advice and the pressure of events.

a) The Incompetence of the Saigon Government

One major cause of escalation was that the Saigon regime was obviously not winning the war. The generals continued to squabble, exasperating the new American ambassador, General Maxwell Taylor. Lodge had had enough by late 1964. All he could suggest was that America should be prepared to run South Vietnam! Despite Taylor's impeccable military pedigree and formidable intellect, he was a poor choice. Johnson picked him to please the JCS, but the situation demanded a real diplomat not an impatient soldier. Taylor treated the Saigon generals like the cadets he once commanded at West Point, the US military academy. In December 1964 he summoned the generals to the US embassy: 'Do all of you understand English?' They nodded. 'I told you all clearly at General Westmoreland's dinner that we Americans were tired of coups. Apparently I wasted my words ... Now you have made a real mess. We cannot carry you forever if you do things like this.' Back in Washington, Dean Rusk was also tired of the South Vietnamese: 'Somehow we must change the pace at which these people move, and I suspect that this can only be done with a pervasive intrusion of Americans into their affairs.' The consensus

among Johnson's advisers was that something must be done, especially when the VC seemed able to strike at will at Americans in South
Vietnam. In November 1964 100 Vietcong dressed in traditional black
peasant pyjamas had attacked and greatly damaged a US air base near
Saigon. The JCS demanded retaliatory air strikes on North Vietnam.
These VC attacks, which the Saigon regime seemed powerless to halt,
nudged the Johnson administration toward escalation. It seemed
necessary for the safety of Americans in Vietnam.

b) The Working Group Recommendations

The presidential election made Johnson cautious about escalation but
he did order a Working Group from the Defence Department, the
State Department, the CIA and the JCS to study Vietnam and suggest
policy options.

The Working Group said an independent and anti-Communist
South Vietnam was vital to America. They reiterated the domino
theory and said that American 'national prestige, credibility, and
honour' were at stake. They emphasised that escalation was necessary
due to the weak Saigon government, which was 'close to a standstill'
and 'plagued by confusion, apathy, and poor morale'. They favoured
heavier bombing, to be halted only if North Vietnam would negotiate.
US terms should be the continued existence of a non-Communist
South Vietnamese government. Thus, although Johnson is blamed
for the escalation, most of those whom David Halberstam bitterly
called 'the best and the brightest' were behind him. Johnson was
commander-in-chief and his military and civilian experts were urging
escalation in the interests of national security. Congress and the
public seemed to be supportive.

An influential minority regretted that insignificant little Vietnam
had taken on such disproportionate significance. George Ball (see
page 44) wanted to concentrate on containing Communism in
Europe. He warned Johnson that the more America got involved in
Vietnam, the harder it would be to get out; that the American public
would not continue to support the war for long. Ball saw no point in
bombing a country with a primarily agricultural economy, with industrial needs served by China and the USSR. Bombing the jungle in
search of VC would be like seeking needles in a haystack. He felt
American soldiers were ineffective in Asiatic jungles and an
increasing American presence was no substitute for good government
in Saigon. He feared that while perseverance proved America's relia-
bility as an ally, it also suggested lack of judgement. He worried about
worldwide reaction to a superpower bombing a tiny Asiatic state.
Both he and Mansfield feared Chinese involvement.

Johnson took the Working Group's recommendations far more
seriously than those of the maverick Ball. In any case, whatever uncertainties existed about the wisdom of escalation were being dispelled

by further VC successes, especially when the security of American bombing bases was at stake.

c) Defending American Bomber Bases with Rolling Thunder

In early 1965 Johnson took the first great escalatory step, when he began large-scale and continuous bombing in Vietnam. Why did he do it?

The immediate trigger for the escalation in 1965 was concern over the security of US bomber bases and personnel. The VC moved freely around South Vietnam, even in the capital, where on Christmas Eve 1964 VC wearing South Vietnamese army uniforms bought on the black market planted a bomb in a bar frequented by American officers. Not wanting any dramatic escalation at Christmas, Johnson did nothing, but events conspired to invite American action. In February 1965, the VC attacked a huge American camp near Pleiku. Eight Americans were killed and one hundred were wounded. Johnson was furious: 'I've had enough of this.' The pressure from his militant advisers was great. Even Ball urged retaliation.

Johnson ordered massively increased air attacks on North Vietnam even though Soviet premier Kosygin was visiting Hanoi. America now moved beyond occasional air-raid reprisals to a limited air war against carefully selected parts of North Vietnam. Such was the intensity of the air strikes that by March they were known as 'Rolling Thunder.' 67 per cent of Americans approved. Bombing the routes taking men and materials to the South would hopefully secure the position of Americans in South Vietnam, decrease infiltration from the north, demoralise Hanoi, and revitalise Saigon where there was some strong middle- and upper-class pressure for negotiations with Hanoi and an end to the bombing.

In February 1965 the *New York Times* said, 'It is time to call a spade a bloody shovel. This country is in an undeclared and unexplained war in Vietnam.' However, Johnson refused to declare war. Why? He feared pressure from his own extreme Cold Warriors: they wanted to go all out, which would jeopardise the financing of the Great Society and lead to increased Soviet or Chinese involvement. 'If one little general in shirtsleeves can take Saigon, think about two hundred million Chinese coming down those trails,' said Johnson. 'No sir! I don't want to fight them.' Johnson assured reporters there was no fear of Chinese intervention because he was seducing rather than raping the North: 'I'm going up her leg an inch at a time.' The next 'inch' would actually be a massive escalation: the commitment of thousands of American ground troops to Vietnam in order to protect the American bomber bases.

d) Defending American Bomber Bases with American Troops

In spring 1965 Johnson made his second great escalatory step when he sent large numbers of American ground troops to Vietnam. Why did he send them?

General William Westmoreland had commanded the 16,000 US 'advisers' in Vietnam since June 1964. In spring 1965 he requested US marines be brought in to protect the vital US bomber base at Danang. Like Lodge before him, Ambassador Taylor warned that once American forces were committed, more would have to be sent in to protect them. He rightly forecast that white Americans would fight no better than the French in Asian jungles and that Americans would be unable to distinguish between a VC and a friendly Vietnamese farmer. He feared Americans would look like colonialists and conquerors and discredit any nationalist credentials of the Saigon regime. Mansfield foresaw thousands of US soldiers going to Vietnam, thereby alienating Congress and world opinion. He rightly pointed out that sending in American ground troops was the way to keep Moscow and Beijing involved. Soviet-designed anti-aircraft defences were already bringing down many American planes.

Johnson ignored those warnings and the first 3,500 marines landed at Danang beach on 8 March 1965, cheered by pretty Vietnamese girls in a welcome arranged by the US navy. On 6 April 1965 Johnson approved an increase of over 18,000 American support forces to keep his soldiers supplied. He also sent in more marines. He said he wanted to avoid 'publicity' and 'minimise any appearance of sudden changes in policy'.

Many accuse Johnson of waging war without a declaration of war. Was it Johnson's undeclared war? Congress supportively granted $700 million for military operations in Vietnam in May 1965. Johnson told them this was no routine grant: it was a vote to continue opposing Communism in Vietnam. The House of Representatives voted 408-7 and the Senate 88-3 in favour. As yet, the majority of American journalists were also hawks, even those like David Halberstam who later became bitterly anti-war. When Vietnam is called 'Johnson's war' this support from Congress and the press at the time of massive escalation should be remembered.

5 Where Are We Going?

Johnson had hoped that the arrival of American troops would help to protect the bomber bases and improve the position of the Saigon regime. However, the situation in Vietnam continued to deteriorate.

In June 1965 General Thieu had become head of state and Air Vice-Marshal Nguyen Cao Ky became prime minister - '... absolutely the bottom of the barrel,' said one Johnson adviser. The son of a small

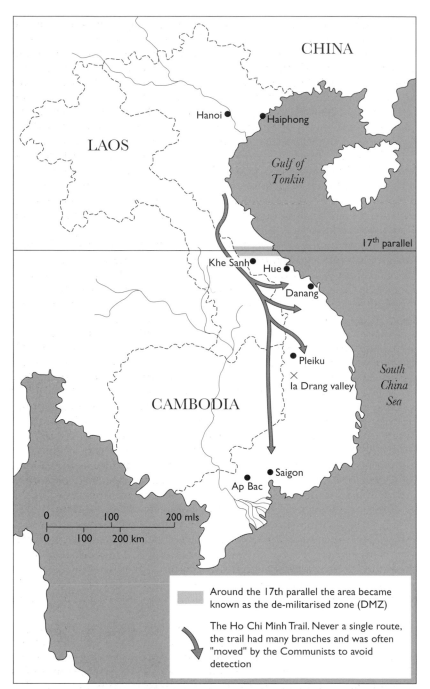

CHINA

Hanoi ●   ● Haiphong

LAOS

Gulf of Tonkin

17th parallel

Khe Sanh ●   ● Hue

● Danang

● Pleiku

× Ia Drang valley

South China Sea

CAMBODIA

0   100   200 mls
0   100   200 km

● Saigon
Ap Bac ●

	Around the 17th parallel the area became known as the de-militarised zone (DMZ)
	The Ho Chi Minh Trail. Never a single route, the trail had many branches and was often "moved" by the Communists to avoid detection

Important places in the American era in Vietnam (c1956-73) landowner, Thieu had served briefly as a village chief under the Vietminh, then decided he would do better in the French colonial army. He became an officer in 1949. Always ambitious, he married into a prominent Vietnamese Catholic family and became a convert. After the French left, the Americans were impressed by his military ability. He was given training in America. He was indecisive, cunning, stubborn, suspicious and corrupt. He often took advice from his personal astrologer. He would plot his way to the presidency in 1967. Ky drank, gambled, and womanised. He said Vietnam needed men like Hitler. Ky had been commander of South Vietnam's air force. He was a flamboyant figure, fond of purple jumpsuits, pearl-handled revolvers and dark sunglasses. At a meeting with McNamara in July 1965, Ky's tight white jacket, shiny black shoes and red socks shocked one American who pointed out that 'at least no one could confuse him with Uncle Ho'.

Ky's government was losing control of territory to the VC who had 75 per cent of the countryside, according to Thieu. As Taylor had feared, the more American troops poured in, the less the ARVN wanted to fight. As usual, Westmoreland demanded more American troops to prevent South Vietnam's collapse and to protect the American troops already there. In cabinet meetings throughout July Johnson expressed doubts about the usefulness of sending more American troops. Nevertheless, on 28 July 1965, at noon when TV audiences were minimal, he announced that Westmoreland had asked for more men to meet mounting Communist aggression and that his needs would be met: 'We will stand in Vietnam.' The 75,000 troops in Vietnam would be increased to 125,000. Congressional leaders had given their assent the day before. During 1965, polls and White House mail showed 70 per cent of the nation was behind Johnson. 80 per cent believed in the domino theory and 80 per cent favoured sending American soldiers to stop South Vietnam falling. Johnson was supported by the majority of Americans in his Vietnam policy. 47 per cent wanted him to send in even more troops. By the end of 1965 nearly 200,000 American soldiers were in Vietnam.

Few were sure this further escalation was the right answer. Protests had begun in the universities in March 1965 (see page 101). Vice-President Hubert Humphrey privately fretted. Why risk Chinese intervention? Why support an unstable country? 'Where are we going?' Johnson himself cried upon hearing a plane had been shot down. He confessed that hawkish General Curtis LeMay 'scares the hell out of me'.

A December 1965 bombing halt failed to persuade Hanoi to negotiate and a cabinet meeting showed the lack of consensus within the administration. George Ball thought the situation hopeless. Maxwell Taylor and the CIA opposed sending more US troops. McNamara felt that military victory was unlikely. The JCS were divided over tactics. 'Tell me this,' said Johnson to the JCS chairman, 'what will happen if we put in 100,000 more men and then two, three years later, you tell me we need 500,000 more? ... And what makes you think that Ho Chi Minh won't put in another 100, and match us every bit of the way?' Johnson knew all the dangers. He was uncertain that America could win, but certain that she could not get out without irreparable damage to his own and his country's position. As American soldiers poured into Vietnam, the administration and military could not agree on what they should be doing there. Most, however, agreed that they SHOULD be there: this was not just Johnson's war.

6 Was it Johnson's War?

Was it Johnson's war? In some ways it seemed as if it was. As president, he made the decision to continue Kennedy's commitment and then to escalate. He ordered each escalatory step, first Rolling Thunder, then the sending of increasing numbers of American troops. On the other hand, many shared the responsibility for all this. He had inherited a strong commitment to South Vietnam from his predecessors with whose Cold War ideas he agreed. In the circumstances of his accession to the presidency, it would have been particularly difficult for him to disengage America from Vietnam, even had he been so inclined. He felt bound to continue Kennedy's policies and keep Kennedy's advisers. When Johnson escalated American involvement in Vietnam dramatically, his military and civilian advisers share responsibility for his policies. He always liked to claim that his responsibility had been shared with Congress and the public and there was a lot of truth in what he said: they WERE clearly supportive of his Vietnam policies early in his presidency. A December 1965 poll showed a large majority of Americans favoured increasing American troops to 500,000 men. Johnson's biographer Vaughn Davis Bornet, while critical of the president's policies, reminds us that,

> If Vietnam did not ultimately go well, in a democratic republic like the United States one must look at the Congress and the people themselves, for three national elections were held during the Johnson years.

Making notes on 'Johnson's War'?

As examiners favour questions on whether Vietnam was Johnson's war, your notes on this chapter should be very detailed, concentrating on why Johnson continued the war, how he was able to escalate, and why he escalated. You could also assess the responsibility of Kennedy, McNamara, Rusk, Congress, the military, the press and the American public for escalation.

Summary Diagram
'Johnson's War'?

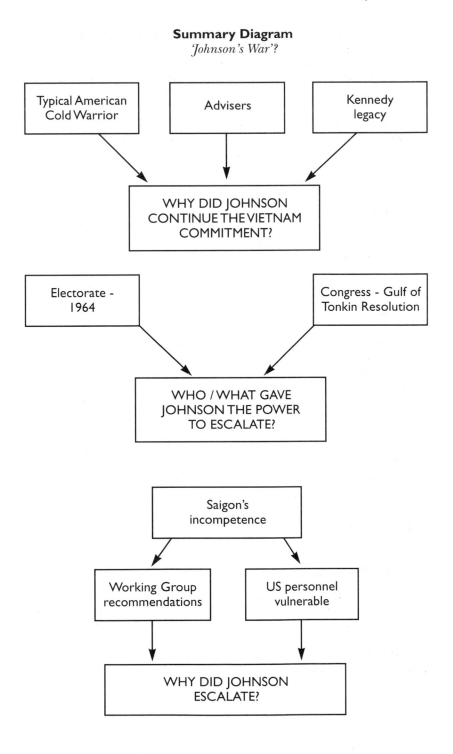

Answering essay questions on 'Johnson's War'?

You are likely to get questions which specifically ask you whether Vietnam was Johnson's war, for example,

1. a) Why did Johnson continue the war? (10 marks)
    b) Why did he escalate? (15 marks)

You might also be asked a far more wide-ranging question such as,

2. Why did America get involved and remain in Vietnam 1950-1968?

All these are quite straightforward 'causes' questions. Sometimes a 'causes' essay question is disguised within a controversial quotation, which you are asked to discuss:

3. 'America's involvement in Vietnam was primarily Johnson's responsibility.' Do you agree?

Examiners penalise candidates who are not relevant. For example, a careless candidate might ignore the dates in Question 2 - explanations of why America was still in Vietnam AFTER 1968 would be irrelevant. One way to remind the examiner you are sticking to the question is by repeating keywords of the question in every paragraph. If the words cannot be easily included in your paragraph it is a sign that you are not answering the question. Experiment with any or all of the above three questions: do the essay(s) or part of the essay(s) and fit in the words of the question in every paragraph. A little variation in the words of the question each time will stop you boring yourself and the examiner. How many different ways can you think of saying 'x ... is why Johnson escalated American involvement'?

Source-based questions on 'Johnson's War'?

Source questions frequently ask you to evaluate the strengths and weaknesses of the source as evidence on a specified topic.

Specimen Question

What are the strengths and weaknesses of Johnson's pre-election promises (page 63) to a historian trying to ascertain whether Johnson planned to escalate once elected? [6 marks]

Specimen Answer

An appropriate answer would be:

Americans still furiously debate whether or not Johnson planned to escalate American involvement in Vietnam once elected. Publicly, Johnson promised the electorate he would not 'send American boys' to do 'what Asian boys ought to be doing', but he had previously (and privately) assured the JCS they could have their war once he was elected. In some respects, neither promise gives the historian strong evidence of Johnson's plans. Both are electioneering promises, and their weakness as evidence is that things which are said to win elections are often forgotten once the election is won. Johnson could have been promising war to the JCS to please the military men or to ensure they did nothing to embarrass him in an election year. On the other hand, he DID escalate after the election. With hindsight, therefore, the historian might consider the promise to the JCS strong evidence that Johnson always planned to escalate. Given that he DID escalate, the historian might then consider that Johnson's promises of peace were simply designed to win the votes of those who did not want to see American men fighting in Vietnam. On the other hand, Johnson's beloved Great Society would be damaged by war and it is likely that he wanted to avoid escalation if it was possible. Both promises therefore have weaknesses as evidence for the historian. Both were probably aimed at winning support, and one promise was subsequently broken. Both promises also have strengths. One promise was actually kept, perhaps telling the historian that Johnson always planned escalation. The other promise fits in with what we know of Johnson's obsession with the Great Society and his uncertainties about Vietnam. Perhaps a strength of both is that they reflect his indecision. [Note that examiners usually choose sources which have both strengths and weaknesses. You should explore both the strengths and weaknesses of both sources, looking at the immediate context and using your background knowledge.]

Now attempt the following questions.

1. The Escalation of American Involvement

Look at the extracts from the State Department expert (page 50), Kennedy (page 50) and the Gulf of Tonkin resolution (page 62). Answer these questions.

a) Explain the references to the Southeast Asia Collective Defence Treaty and a 'protocol state' in the resolution. (2 marks)

b) What did the State Department expert expect the others to have learned from 'the past' about the combination of 'nationalism and Communism' in Vietnam? (2 marks)

c) Judging from the second and third sources, in what ways had American ideas on how to win in Vietnam changed? (3 marks)

d) Judging from the content and tone, what kind of case was America aiming to present in the resolution? (5 marks)

e) What are the strengths and weaknesses of the Gulf of Tonkin resolution as an explanation of why America was now apparently prepared to use armed force in Vietnam? (6 marks)

f) Using the sources and your background knowledge, explain why Johnson escalated American involvement in 1965. (7 marks)

6 Living and Fighting in Vietnam

The last chapter looked at one great debate about Johnson and Vietnam. Why did he continue and escalate the involvement? The other great debate concerns the reasons why Johnson's America (and its South Vietnamese ally) was unable to defeat the Communists. Despite Johnson's dramatic escalation of the American war effort, his advisers concluded that the war was unwinnable and Johnson began to retreat in 1968.

General Giap said Hanoi won because it waged a people's war, a total war in which every man, woman and even child was mobilised. He maintained that human beings were the decisive factor. This chapter will concentrate on ordinary people living and fighting in Vietnam, and provide some answers to both of the major questions relating to Johnson's presidency.

1 The Press

Journalists and photographers from all over the world flocked to and fed upon Vietnam. War makes good news: the public are interested in the drama of death. War images are a gift to writers and photographers. Some of the best war photographs were taken in Vietnam: helicopters whirring over peasants in fields, shell-shocked faces or wounded bodies are very dramatic.

There is no doubt that many members of the press corps got high on the war. The British photographer Tim Page was wounded twice in Vietnam. He left but could not resist returning for the Tet offensive. In 1969 an American sergeant in front of him stepped on a mine. A long piece of shrapnel blew away brain tissue the size of an orange. Page tried to take more photos then collapsed. A British publisher asked him to write a book to 'take the glamour out of war'. Page said no one could: it was fun, like sex and the Rolling Stones. He thought the pressmen liked the brush with that which was most evil, most dear, most profane. They liked the camaraderie and the sheer adventure of it all. Page felt sorry for the Vietnamese 'whose country had become our adventure sandbox'. Page helps us understand the attraction of war to some of the military and why so many Americans volunteered to fight in Vietnam. Michael Herr was a journalist. His book *Dispatches* is an eloquent, dramatic, novelistic, self-consciously well-written account of his time reporting in Vietnam. He felt that he and the soldiers had watched too many war films all their lives, so that seeing real war and real death did not have the full impact. Everything seemed unreal, like a scene from a movie. Herr felt the press were probably 'glorified war-profiteers', 'thrill freaks, death-wishers, wound-seekers, ghouls'. Perhaps some of us who write and read about war are similar.

In the work of the world's press on Vietnam we can see one of the great causes of the war, the romance and heroism which attracts many civilians and soldiers. We can also see one of the main reasons why America lost the war: the press coverage upset many Americans. Their writings and photographs showed up the horrors and truths about the war which are covered in the remainder of this chapter.

2 The Vietnamese

Studying the war from the viewpoint of the ordinary Vietnamese helps explain why the Communists triumphed.

a) Winning the Hearts and Minds of the People

Most Vietnamese were peasants, usually living in small villages, on the irrigated plains alongside the great northern Red River and the south's Mekong River. Their main crop was rice and whole families worked long hours in the rice fields. The villages lacked electricity. The houses had dirt or wooden floors. The dirt paths between the houses were piled with stinking human and animal ordure for fertil ising the fields. The small homes were made of mud and bamboo with roofs of palm leaves or grass. The families slept on reed mattresses on the ground. There was no running water. American soldiers could not conceive of 'real' people living like this, and the resultant sense of an alien world goes a little way toward explaining why Americans some- times treated the Vietnamese peasants as sub-human and were conse- quently unable to win many of them over to their side.

The peasants had always been used to struggling to provide suffi- cient food for their families, and this had led to an emphasis upon collective discipline and endeavour. Harvesting was best approached communally. Within the family and the village individual interests were frequently subordinated to community interests. Many villages adapted with relative ease to the principles of Communism and to the fraternal leadership of cadres, who chivvied, inspired and monitored the people. The Communists worked hard to win over the peasantry, offering them a fairer distribution of land and urging Communist soldiers to avoid the rape and pillage characteristic of the ARVN. Although the Communists were generally better at winning the hearts and minds of the peasantry, they were ruthless when necessary. During the Tet offensive, the VC dragged 'unfriendly' people out of their houses in Hue and shot them, clubbed them to death, or buried them alive. 3,000 bodies were found in the river or jungle. A judicious mixture of ruthlessness and frequent good behaviour gained the VC the sullen acquiescence or support of the peasants which was vital in guerrilla warfare. Giap's strategy was to use the Vietcong for incessant guerrilla warfare to wear down Saigon and its American allies, while the NVA would only fight conventional set-piece battles at times and places when it was sufficiently strong. This emphasis upon guerrilla warfare meant that the Communists needed (and usually obtained) a great deal of support from South Vietnam's civilians. Villagers often gave them the food, shelter and hiding places necessary for survival. Success in winning the hearts and minds of the peasants helps explain why the Communists defeated Washington and Saigon.

The actions of both Washington and Saigon frequently antagonised the South Vietnamese peasants, helping to explain America's failure. Life for the South Vietnamese peasantry deteriorated from bad to worse after the Americans arrived. Diem's strategic hamlets programme and then American bombing forced many peasants to move away from the homes, crops and ancestral graves which meant so much to them. One peasant recalled a day when

1   The bombing started at about eight o'clock in the morning and lasted for hours. When we first heard the explosions, we rushed into the tunnels, but not everyone made it. When there was a pause in the attack, some of us climbed out to see what we could do, and the scene
5   was terrifying. Bodies had been torn to pieces - limbs were hanging from trees and scattered around the ground. The bombing began again, this time with napalm, and the village went up in flames. The napalm hit me. I felt as if I were burning all over, like a piece of coal. I lost consciousness. Friends took me to the hospital, and my wounds didn't begin to
10 heal until six months later. Over two hundred people died in the raid, including my mother, sister-in-law and three nephews. They were buried alive when their tunnel collapsed.

Ironically, American firepower was concentrated more on South than North Vietnam. The dependent Saigon regime was unlikely to complain. Johnson usually tried to avoid targeting non-combatants, saying 'if they [the US pilots] hit people I'll bust their asses'. However, in their search for VC the Americans killed and wounded tens of thousands of civilians who might or might not have been Communist sympathisers. Neither the American army nor the ARVN would take responsibility for wounded civilians who were left to get what (if any) primitive medical care was available. Bombing obliterated five towns with populations over 10,000, and many villages. Some civilians lived like moles in caves and tunnels, emerging to work but ready to go back down when planes appeared. Children were kept down for days at a time. Bombing was not the way to win people over.

American technology created formidable new fighting weapons. The Vietnamese called cluster bombs 'mother bombs' because after exploding in mid-air they released 350-600 baby bombs. Each one exploded on impact into thousands of metal pellets. Later, fibreglass replaced the metal; X-rays could not detect it and it was harder and more painful to remove. Heat-sensitive and urine-sniffing devices were developed to pinpoint and destroy an enemy, but this often turned out to be a water buffalo or a child. An American pilot

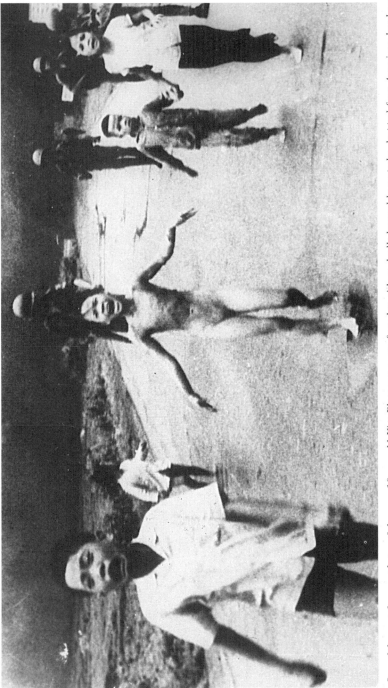

One of the most famous photos of the war: 10-year-old Kim Phuc ran away from her village, badly burned by napalm dropped from American bombers

described the effectiveness of the new white phosphorous:

1 We sure are pleased with those back room boys at Dow [Chemical Company]. The original product wasn't so hot - if the gooks [Vietnamese] were quick they could scrape it off. So the boys started adding polystyrene - now it sticks like shit to a blanket. But then if the
5 gooks jumped under water it stopped burning, so they started adding Willie Peter [WP - white phosphorous] so's to make it burn better. It'll even burn under water now. And one drop is enough, it'll keep on burning right down to the bone so they die anyway from phosphorous poisoning.

It was very difficult for the Americans to win the hearts and minds of the people and the war when their military tactics aroused such antagonism. One Vietnamese nun told an American relief worker that Vietnam was a beautiful country 'until YOU arrived'.

b) Communist Determination, Heroism and Ingenuity

Inspired by Communism and nationalism, the VC won admiration from their American foes. One American general was impressed by some besieged Communists in a bunker, who 'didn't even give up after their eardrums had burst from the concussion [from American fire-power] … and blood was pouring out of their noses'. Unable to afford uniform changes, the VC suffered from skin diseases because of the wet conditions in jungles, rice fields and tunnels. They picked up infections from insect bites, dirty water, and dead bodies in the soil. Quinine was in short supply and all had malaria. The Vietnamese had always struggled for their existence against both nature and other, hostile races. Continuous struggle ensured unusual patience in the face of adversity. This helps explain Hanoi's refusal to be beaten. As Giap said,

> We were not strong enough to drive out a half million American troops, but that was not our aim. Our intention was to break the will of the American government to continue the war.

America did not understand that determination. American strategy never took it into account, and this was an important factor in the American defeat.

Most of Giap's men and women spent time on the Ho Chi Minh Trail which came southward via Cambodia and Laos. Both sides knew that keeping the trail open was vital to the Communist war effort. Men and materials came south and the wounded were sent north on the trail. Giap's people used bulky pack bicycles with rag-stuffed tyres that did not burst. Many were full-time porters on the trail and an estimated 10 per cent of them died, mostly from amoebic dysentery and malaria. A man could carry 55 pounds of rice or 40 pounds of other materials (the rice bags moulded themselves to the body and were

People power in action. Hanoi kept supplies moving south, on bikes if necessary

easier to carry) over 15 miles by day or 12 by night. Human portage lasted from 1959 to 1964 when the trail was widened and sometimes even covered with asphalt to accommodate big vehicles. It was never a single route. There were several branches, along which were dotted repair workshops, stores depots, hospitals and rest camps. Around 50,000 women were employed at any one time to repair the road. If one part was damaged by American bombing, the traffic would be switched to other branches while repairs were done. Vehicles and parts of the trail were camouflaged with foliage. Giap's trails, troops, and trucks melted into the landscape. The Soviets and Chinese provided thousands of cheap trucks. Hanoi lost many $6,000 trucks, but America lost many several million dollar bombers. American bombers perpetually sought to obliterate the trail but failed. In 1967 the Americans dropped seismic sensors on the ground so that aircraft could target trail users. Vietnam's elephant population was badly depleted by the resultant bombing. When the VC saw the sensors they deliberately triggered them off with recorded cassettes then disappeared. The battle of the trail was a vital one, in which people could be said to have triumphed over technology.

In autumn 1965 the 66th regiment of the NVA went south on the trail. Each soldier had a khaki uniform, a pair of sandals cut from old tyres, and ankle-high green canvas Chinese boots. Each carried 22 pounds of food for the two month walk from North Vietnam to the Ia Drang Valley. The weapons they carried were made in Albania, China, Czechoslovakia and the USSR. Each soldier took a daily malaria pill but most got the disease anyway. Several died on the trail each day, from disease, accidents, snake bites or American air raids. In November they clashed with the US army. In the 34-day Battle of Ia Drang, 305 Americans and 3,561 North Vietnamese died. Both sides thought they had won, that the other would not be able to sustain such losses. It was the North Vietnamese who were eventually proved right. Ia Drang is a good illustration of the Communist determination which helped ensure their ultimate victory.

Communist ingenuity and preparedness was vitally important. In many areas supposedly subject to the Saigon government there was a highly efficient Communist underground organisation. The Communist party had a web of informants and a multitude of social organisations which helped comfort, control and motivate the people in uncertain times. The Communist network of tunnels in which VC could hide, shelter and regroup was literally underground. In January 1967 the Americans found a maze of tunnels north of Saigon. These were like an underground city, full of stoves, furniture, clothing and paperwork. An exploring American officer was killed by a booby trap so the Americans just pumped in tear gas, set off explosives, then got out. They had just missed the VC headquarters, several miles of tunnels away. In Hanoi itself the government made excellent preparations against air raids. The ground was riddled with concrete boltholes, each with a thick concrete cover which could be pulled over the top. When the sirens sounded, most of Hanoi's population could vanish. Two million northerners, mostly women, were in the 'Shock Brigades' which repaired the effects of air-raid damage to roads and railways. Communist determination, heroism and ingenuity were all vital to the American defeat.

c) Corruption, Decay and Saigon

Studying corruption and decay in the South (especially in Saigon) is important for understanding the outcome of the war.

Incessant fighting and bombing drove millions of peasants out of the countryside into the towns and cities. By 1968 roughly one third of South Vietnam's population had been relocated. Many were put up in camps where primitive sanitation bred disease. Many lived off Americans, particularly in Saigon. Saigon was where Americans and Vietnamese met and mixed most.

Mid-twentieth-century Saigon was still a strange and lovely mixture of Southeast Asia and provincial France. Its tree-shaded streets were lined with quiet shops and sleepy pavement cafes. The beautiful villas of the residential districts had lush tropical gardens of yellow scented jasmine and mimosa and purple and red bougainvillaea. It became an unsavoury city in the American war years. Drugs were sold in its bars. Many hotels were brothels. The streets were awash with black market goods, American soldiers, orphans, cripples, beggars, and 56,000 registered prostitutes. The beggars targeted 'rich' Americans, tugging at them and making crying sounds. On the beautiful tiled terrace of the French colonial-style Continental Palace Hotel in Saigon, limbless Vietnamese victims of the war crawled crab-like along the floor seeking handouts from Americans. The war had destroyed the social fabric of South Vietnam, uprooting peasants to the cities, and dividing families. Poor peasant girls who turned to prostitution dismayed their families, despite earning more in a week than the whole family did in a year. American dollars distorted the economy. The salary of the lowest ranking American was gigantic by Vietnamese standards. Taxi drivers would not stop for other Vietnamese if it was possible to be hailed by an American. Vietnamese professionals lost status and influence in this new dollar-dominated world. A Vietnamese waiter serving big-tipping Americans would earn more than his doctor father. Garbage and sewage disposal suffered as municipal workers sought higher wages working for Americans. On one pavement pile of rat-covered garbage was a sign 'THIS IS THE FRUIT OF AMERICAN AID.'

Saigon was full of Vietnamese and American officials. There was much talk but little real communication. The Americans would put forward plans and, so long as America financed them, the Vietnamese would agree although not necessarily co-operate. A cynical American official described how things worked:

1   Say, for instance, that we hand them a plan to distribute ten thousand
  radios to villages so that peasants can listen to Saigon propaganda
  broadcasts. They respond enthusiastically, and we deliver the radios. A
  few months later, when we inquire, they tell us what we want to hear:
5   peasants are being converted to the government cause, and we're
  winning the war. But what has really happened? Have all the radios
  reached the villages, or have half of them been sold on the black market?
  Are peasants listening to Saigon or to Hanoi? We don't know. We're in
  the mysterious East. We report progress to Washington because
10 Washington demands progress.

American aid rarely reached the peasants for whom it was primarily
intended. Much of it found its way into the pockets of the military and
urban elites. Even when American fertiliser got to the countryside, it
was hoarded, and artificially created shortages caused the price to
rise: Thieu's brother-in-law was a leading speculator. Thieu himself
carried away millions of dollars in gold when he fled Vietnam in April
1975. Theft from the Americans was extensive: American products
were stolen and sold on street corners, even rifles and ammunition.
Whole consignments disappeared without trace. An investigation
revealed that the amount of cement supposedly needed by and given
to Vietnamese officials in one year could have paved over the whole
country. The endemic corruption owed much to the Vietnamese
emphasis on family duty. Poorly paid officials and even the highly
paid president wanted to provide well for their relations. Thieu's
cousin ran a wealthy province: for a fee he would let VC out of jail or
keep ARVN men out of battle. One wonders whether the anti-
Communist Vietnamese would have stood more of a chance of success
had they not been distracted by the incredible temptations of
American largesse or disoriented by the impact of the American
presence.

d) The ARVN

South Vietnam was never well governed under Diem and his successors. The corruption and mismanagement that characterised South
Vietnam's government naturally permeated its armed forces. Many
military leaders were political appointees and fought accordingly. The
high command spent more time fighting among themselves than
against the enemy. Saigon wanted to avoid losses. In February 1971,
30,000 ARVN invaded Laos with orders to retreat if over 3,000 died.
They retreated, halfway to their objective. The Americans described
their own tactics as 'Search and Destroy' but those of the ARVN as
'Search and Avoid'. Poor results decreased confidence in a vicious
circle. Units were unwilling to engage the enemy if the astrological
signs were against it or if great losses seemed likely. The urban middle-

class officers did not get on well with the peasants in the lower ranks. 80 per cent of South Vietnamese were Buddhist but only 5 per cent of the ARVN leadership were. ARVN wages were so low that by 1966 the soldiers depended on American surplus rice. Some ARVN officers sold American cigarettes, whiskey, rifles, ammunition, uniforms, boots and helmets on the black market. Others pocketed the pay of thousands of deserters, sick or dead men. Lower ranks bullied and robbed the population. A high proportion deserted to the Communists. On the other hand, because they were not always able to call on air support or helicopters to evacuate their wounded, the ARVN was often remarkably tenacious when cornered. Many ARVN fought often and bravely, and tens of thousands of them died.

The ARVN were compromised in the eyes of the Vietnamese people by their association with the Americans, while Americans such as Westmoreland were frequently unwilling to use ARVN assistance because they despised them and because any military leader is more at ease with his own men. In Westmoreland's headquarters in Saigon there were hidden nozzles to spray his 'elite' ARVN guards with tear gas if they defected. Relations between the American forces and the ARVN were never very good. After the disastrous battle of Ap Bac (see page 44) American pilots sang new words to the tune 'On Top of Old Smokey':

> We were supporting the ARVNs,
> A group without guts,
> Attacking a village
> Of straw-covered huts.
> The VCs start shooting,
> They fire a big blast,
> We off-load the ARVNs
> They sit on their ass.
> An armoured battalion
> Just stayed in a trance,
> One captain died trying
> To make them advance.
> When the news was reported
> The ARVNs had won,
> The VCs are laughing
> Over their captured guns.

The morale and performance of the ARVN is a major factor in explaining the defeat of the Washington-Saigon alliance.

3 The Americans

Of the 26.8 million American men of fighting age in the 1960s, 10.93 million served in the military; 2.2 million were drafted but 8.7 million were volunteers, many inspired by a sense of duty, patriotism, family tradition or a belief in the rectitude of America's cause. This is well illustrated in *Born on the Fourth of July*, the autobiography of Ron Kovic. The book was made into an impressive film starring Tom Cruise as Kovic. Raised on a diet of Second World War movies, playing boyhood war games, believing Communists to be ungodly and evil, Kovic joined up when marine recruiters came to his high school. They reminded him of John Wayne, whose name frequently recurs in the history of the Vietnam war (Johnson hoped Wayne would play him in any film of his life). When interviewed many said they were inspired by Hollywood movies. One said he was influenced by the 'John Wayne syndrome'. Another thought he would be 'a soldier like John Wayne … who feared nothing and either emerged with the medals and the girl, or died heroically'. Others joined for different reasons. Robert Mason's *Chickenhawk* is the well-written memoir of a helicopter pilot in Vietnam who says he joined up just because he wanted to fly. Mason claims he knew nothing then of what the war was about. A platoon leader suggested another motive: 'It turned out that most of us liked to kill other men.' Looking back, a high proportion of veterans said they were glad to have fought in Vietnam, and enjoyed their time there. Factors such as duty, patriotism and even enjoyment of war help explain why many American men fought in Vietnam. American disunity, the insistence upon a 'comfortable' war, and problems particular to fighting in Vietnam help explain why these men were unable to defeat the Communists.

a) American Disunity

Although many Americans fought with conviction and bravery, the American and allied forces were frequently disunited. The marines were traditionally linked with the navy and were not keen to obey orders from Westmoreland's army. The unconventional Green Berets aroused antagonism. Americans distrusted the ARVN. At Khe Sanh (see page 99) in 1968, Westmoreland sent for ARVN representation as an afterthought, and then deployed them somewhere unimportant. Ordinary soldiers served 365 days, marines 13 months. Many stencilled the return dates on their helmets. This short term of service meant that units never attained the *esprit de corps* vital to morale and performance. 13 per cent of Americans in Vietnam were black but a disproportionate 28 per cent were in combat units, which naturally led to resentment. Many American soldiers did not like their country's manner of waging war. Others felt America had no right to intervene in Vietnam. In 1966 an ex-Green Beret said he doubted Vietnam would be better off under Ho's Communism, 'but it is not for me or my government to decide. That decision is for the Vietnamese.' Some disapproved of the mistreatment of civilians on humanitarian or military grounds. Disagreement with the war or tactics led to indiscipline. An underground newspaper offered a

$10,000 bounty for the death of the officer responsible for Hamburger Hill (see page 87). Things got much worse under Johnson's successor. In 1969 an entire company sat down on the battlefield, while in full view of TV cameras another refused to go down a dangerous trail.

In the late 1960s anti-war feeling grew in America. Many American soldiers became confused about what they were fighting for. Many returned home to find themselves ostracised, jeered, and spat on as they wore their uniform. Some found the families they had left at home had been victimised by opponents of the war. Homes belonging to soldiers might have broken glass spread across their lawns, or objects thrown at their windows. In the Second World War the folks back home cheered you as you worked your way toward Berlin or Japan. In Vietnam you fought for ground, won it, and left knowing the VC would move in again. Meanwhile, the folks back home called you 'baby-killer'. The collapse of the home front (see pages 100-104) was a crucial factor in America's failure in Vietnam. It damaged troop morale and hamstrung the government in Washington.

b) Trying to Fight a 'Comfortable' War

Ironically, the American desire to keep their soldiers as comfortable as possible in Vietnam helps to explain their defeat there. President Nixon said,

1   If we fail it will be because the American way simply isn't as effective as the Communist way ... I have an uneasy feeling that this may be the case. We give them the most modern arms, we emphasise the material to the exclusion of the spiritual and the Spartan life, and it may be that
5   we soften them up rather than harden them up for the battle.

Many soldiers never actually fought. They had to organise the American lifestyle for everyone else - running clubs, cinemas and PXs (post exchanges). The main PX in Saigon was larger than a New York department store and contained almost as much - jewellery, perfume, alcohol, sports clothes, cameras, tape recorders, radios, soap, shampoo, deodorant, condoms. Every week, several thousand combat soldiers were sent for R and R (rest and recuperation) to Saigon or Japan. All this led to an air of unreality and disorientation. A soldier could be airlifted from the horrors of the jungle to a luxurious air-conditioned base so cold there were homely fireplaces. He could have steak, French fries, ice cream and Coca-Cola. Sometimes cigarettes and iced beer were dropped by helicopters in mid-siege, and hot meals were landed at remote jungle camps. One colonel got a Silver Star bravery award for delivering turkeys by helicopter for Thanksgiving. When the last American soldier left Vietnam, there were 357 American libraries, 159 basketball courts, 90 service clubs, 85 volleyball fields, 71 swimming pools, 55 softball fields, 40 ice-cream plants, 30 tennis courts and two bowling alleys. The American soldier was fighting a different war from his enemy. Every soldier suffers great personal hardship in the field but while many North Vietnamese and VC spent years away from their families, existed on a basic diet and lacked decent medical treatment, the typical American soldier served a short term in Vietnam, and had good food and medical treatment. One NVA soldier thought this was the difference between the two sides:

> 1 You ask me what I thought of the Americans. We thought the Americans were handsome soldiers but looked as if they were made with flour ... it was difficult for them to suffer all the hardships of the Vietnamese battlefront. When we had no water to drink, they had water for
> 5 showers! We could suffer the hardships much better than they could. That probably was the main reason we won.

Westmoreland said this was the only way you could get Americans to fight.

Frustration with the war led many American soldiers to seek comfort elsewhere. In 1966 there were around 30,000 war-orphaned child prostitutes, but they could not cope with the American demand. Around a quarter of American soldiers caught sexually transmitted diseases. Drug abuse became common. In 1970 an estimated 58 per cent of Americans in Vietnam smoked 'pot' (marijuana), 22 per cent shot up heroin. One colonel was court-marshalled for leading his squadron in pot parties. In 1971 5,000 needed treatment for combat wounds, 20,529 for serious drug abuse. It was hard to take action over the drug market as so many prominent government officials in Saigon were involved, including Ky. It was hard to win a war when army discipline deteriorated: the process began under Johnson, then accelerated under his successor.

c) Problems for the Officers

Americans of different ranks had different experiences. An American army officer did five months in the front line. He would probably be less experienced than some of the soldiers he commanded. Five months was too little to get to know his men properly. He would then be moved on to a training, organisation or a desk job. Unpopular officers were shot in the back in action or had fragmentation grenades thrown at them. Under Johnson's successor, between 1969 and 1971, there were 730 'fraggings', killing 83 officers. Often they were simply trying to get their men to fight. It was hard to win a war with so many inexperienced and increasingly unpopular officers.

d) Problems for the 'Grunts'

The young foot soldier or 'grunt' like Ron Kovic was often horrified by what he saw in 'Nam' and was keen to get out. Many hoped for a small wound and some shot themselves in the foot. What was so awful about this war?

The average age of the grunt in Vietnam was 19, compared to a less vulnerable 26 in the Second World War. To make matters worse, there seemed to be no progress being made, as is illustrated in another evocative film, *Hamburger Hill*. The film told the true story of the bloody May 1969 attempt to gain a hill which was quickly retaken by the VC. Any time the Americans or ARVN moved out of an area, the Communists would move in. The grunt never felt safe. 20 per cent of American wounded were victims of booby traps rather than direct enemy fire. There were booby traps all around, including the 'Bouncing Betty' which shot out of the earth and exploded after being stepped on. Explosions blew away limbs. The VC wired up dead bodies with mines and camouflaged holes on trails so Americans would fall in and be impaled on sharpened bamboo stakes. These were positioned so the victim could not get out without tearing off flesh. The patrolling infantryman was thus in almost continuous danger, with enemy mines, booby traps or snipers likely to get him at any time. Sweat-drenched grunts hated the physical problems of patrolling the ground. They carried 50-70 pounds of equipment, and were plagued by heat, rain and insects:

> We were covered with inch-long fire ants. They bit everything they landed on, and by the time we had sprayed DDT down each other's backs and finally killed them, we were all burning from the bites and the DDT.

The heat was often suffocating, making breathing difficult. Salt tablets were chewed to counter sweat loss. In the paddy fields metal gun parts burned in the sun. In the jungle thick foliage blotted out the sun and moving air, and thorn scratches bled. Uniforms rotted because of the dampness.

Not knowing which Vietnamese were the enemy was the worse thing. That was one of the biggest and most demoralising differences from the Second World War. One admiral said:

> 1 We should have fought in the north, where everyone was the enemy, where you didn't have to worry whether or not you were shooting friendly civilians. In the south, we had to cope with women concealing grenades in their brassieres, or in their baby's diapers. I remember two
> 5 of our marines being killed by a youngster who they were teaching to play volleyball.

A soldier recalled:

> 1 You never knew who was the enemy and who was the friend. They all looked alike. They all dressed alike. They were all Vietnamese. Some of them were Vietcong. Here's a [young] women ... She is pregnant, and she tells an interrogator that her husband works in Danang and isn't a

5   Vietcong. But she watches your men walk down a trail and get killed or
     wounded by a booby trap. She knows the booby trap is there, but she
     doesn't warn them. Maybe she planted it herself ... The enemy was all
     around you.

It was hard to win the war when many of the grunts were terrified and
demoralised.

e) Poor Relationships with Civilians

One of the main reasons the Americans could not defeat the
Communists was because they were unable to win the hearts and
minds of the people. There were thousands of American civilian
'experts' in Vietnam during the war. By mid 1964 there were helpful
Americans in the provinces teaching the Vietnamese to breed pigs,
dig wells and build houses. There were American doctors, school-
teachers, accountants, mechanics and the DJs running the American
radio station in Saigon, as portrayed in the Robin Williams film *Good
Morning Vietnam.* Civilian and military experts frequently clashed.
Civilian experts felt insufficient was done to win the hearts and
minds of the people. Understandably, the military men thought in
terms of force. The circumstances of the war tended to make
American soldiers dislike the people they were supposed to be
helping, which then made it very difficult to win the war.

In 1965 some marines were supposed to search hamlets for VC and
dispense food and medical care, but one marine remembered differently:

1   We would go through a village before dawn, rousting everybody out of
     bed and kicking down doors and dragging them out if they didn't move
     fast enough. They all had underground bunkers inside their huts to
     protect themselves against bombing and shelling. But to us the bunkers
5   were Vietcong hiding places, and we'd blow them up with dynamite - and
     blow up their huts too. If we spotted extra rice lying around, we'd
     confiscate it to keep them from giving it to the Vietcong. [The peasants
     were] herded like cattle into a barbed wire compound, and left to sit
     there in the hot sun for the rest of the day, with no shade. [South
10   Vietnamese policemen and an American interrogator would question
     some peasants about the VC presence in the area.] If they had the
     wrong identity card, or if the police held a grudge against them, they'd
     be beaten pretty badly, maybe tortured. Or they might be hauled off to
     jail, and God knows what happened to them. At the end of the day, the
15   villagers would be turned loose. Their homes had been wrecked, their
     rice confiscated - and if they weren't pro-Vietcong before we got there,
     they sure as hell were by the time we left.

A marine recalled approaching a village which supported the VC:

> Our guys were falling everywhere ... We were pinned down, all day and all night ... we just lay there, waiting and waiting and hearing our partners dying, big guys dying and crying for their mothers, asking to be shot because they couldn't take it no more.

When the marine's unit finally entered the village only old men and women remained, denying any connection with the VC. The marine recalled:

> Our emotions were very low because we'd lost a lot of friends ... So ... we gave it to them ... whatever was moving was going to move no more - especially after [our] 3 days of blood and guts in the mud.

Success could not be measured by territorial gain, so the emphasis was on enemy body counts. More bodies meant more promotions, medals, R and R and rations. You invented dead bodies or you created them: 'If it's dead and Vietnamese, it's VC.' The most famous but by no means the only example of American hatred of the Vietnamese was the massacre at apparently pro-Communist My Lai on 16 March 1968. 347 unarmed civilians were beaten and killed by American soldiers and their officers: old men, women, teenagers and even babies. Women were beaten with rifle butts, raped, and shot. Water buffalo, pigs and chickens were shot then dropped in wells to poison the water.

War inevitably bred brutality. In 1968 the CIA introduced a system code-named 'Operation Phoenix' whereby tens of thousands of VC were sought out and interrogated. Few taken for interrogation came out alive. Torture was the norm. An American officer testified before Congress about the methods used:

> 1 the insertion of the 6-inch dowel into the canal of one of my detainee's ears and the tapping through the brain until he died. The starving to death [in a cage] of a Vietnamese woman who was suspected of being a ... cadre ... the use of electronic gear ... attached to ... both the
> 5 women's vagina and the men's testicles [to] shock them into submission.

American attitudes to the Vietnamese made it difficult to win them over and thereby win the war. Many Americans considered the Vietnamese peasants in particular as less than human. When asked about civilian casualties Westmoreland agreed it was a problem, 'but it does deprive the enemy of the population, doesn't it? They are Asians who don't think about death the way we do.' Maxwell Taylor admitted before he died that Americans never really knew or understood any of the Vietnamese. Helicopters and fire power were no substitute for working amongst and winning over the people.

Americans still argue today about the Communist victory in Vietnam. Was it inevitable? Are guerrillas impossible to beat when much of the population is sympathetic to them? Or was it just that the Americans were not the people to win this war? Were American tactics

wrong? Was Westmoreland's war of attrition the way to defeat determined nationalists and guerrillas? Should America have concentrated
upon winning the hearts and minds of the people? Were bombing
and 'search [for Communists] and destroy' tactics wise? Did the
American public lose the war for America? Or the American media?
Or American politicians? This chapter will probably have made up
your mind about the answer to those questions which centre upon
events in Vietnam. The next chapter will give you more ideas about
the 'home front' and the loss of the war.

Making notes on 'Living and Fighting in Vietnam'

The reasons why America lost the war are a popular topic amongst
examiners, so your notes on this chapter should be detailed. Your
notes could take the form of a list of reasons why the Communists
won. You might decide to concentrate upon similarities and/or differences between the American and Communist i) approaches to
winning the hearts and minds of the people, ii) military strategy, iii)
commitment, iv) problems and solutions to them.

Source-based questions on 'Living and Fighting in Vietnam'

Source-based questions frequently ask you to interpret a source by
studying its style or tone. An example of this is given below.

Specimen Question
What is the American official's attitude (see page 82) towards the
Vietnamese people? Refer to the content and tone of his comments in
your answer. (5 marks)

Specimen Answer
One appropriate answer would be:
   The official has a sceptical attitude to the efficiency and honesty of
America's Vietnamese allies: 'they respond enthusiastically', but just
'tell us what we want to hear'. The rather sarcastic and cynical tone of
those comments suggests that at the very least he is exasperated with
the allies and perhaps even has a rather hostile attitude to them. He
affects an uncomprehending attitude to 'the mysterious East', an old-
fashioned cliché reflecting traditional white racist attitudes to
Orientals. The use of that old cliché might simply suggest a cynical attitude toward the Vietnamese but might conceivably indicate that this
official does not really like them. It may be that he is cynical rather than
hostile because his attitude to Washington is similar - 'Washington
demands progress' he says in a resigned tone, so he reports progress. [A
good answer will repeatedly use the words 'attitude' and 'tone' and
quote briefly from the source to prove the writer's point.]
   Now attempt the questions on page 92.

Summary Diagram
'Living and Fighting in Vietnam'

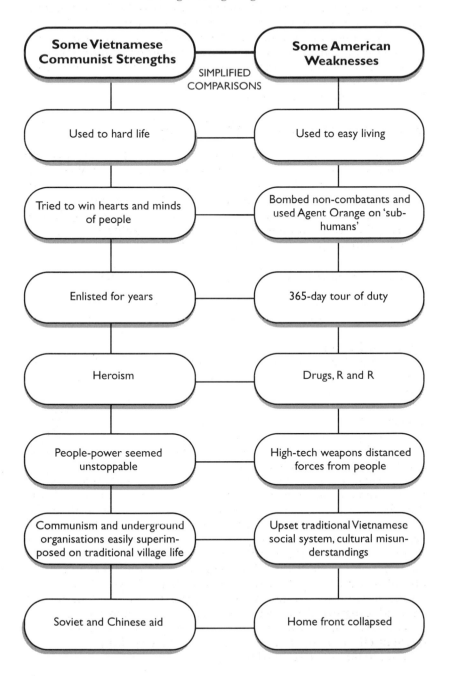

Some Vietnamese Communist Strengths — SIMPLIFIED COMPARISONS — Some American Weaknesses

Used to hard life — Used to easy living

Tried to win hearts and minds of people — Bombed non-combatants and used Agent Orange on 'sub-humans'

Enlisted for years — 365-day tour of duty

Heroism — Drugs, R and R

People-power seemed unstoppable — High-tech weapons distanced forces from people

Communism and underground organisations easily superimposed on traditional village life — Upset traditional Vietnamese social system, cultural misunderstandings

Soviet and Chinese aid — Home front collapsed

1. Americans in Vietnam

Look at the sources on pages 76, 78, 88 and 89. Answer the following questions.

a) Who were:
  (i) the ARVN? (1 mark)
  (ii) the VC? (1 mark)

b) How and why do the attitudes of:
  (i) the wounded peasant,
  (ii) the American pilot and
  (iii) the two American marines differ in their discussion of the deaths of Vietnamese civilians? (4 marks)

c) Using the tone and content of the source to justify your choice, explain which American source you consider to be most sympathetic to the Vietnamese. (5 marks)

d) What are the advantages and disadvantages of sources such as the American pilot to a historian studying Americans in Vietnam? (6 marks)

e) Using these sources and your background knowledge, explain how Americans strategy and behaviour in Vietnam helped the Communist victory. (8 marks)

7 Johnson's Failure

When Johnson became president in 1963 he and his advisers were confident that America could 'win' in Vietnam. 'Winning' required the defeat of the Communists in South Vietnam and the sustaining of a strong and independent state there. However, by the time Johnson's presidency drew to an end, most of his advisers believed that the war was unwinnable and/or that America would have to dramatically change its approach, maybe even get out of Vietnam altogether.

We have seen that one of the great debates about Johnson's presidency centres on why he could not win the war in Vietnam. Chapter 6 concentrated upon the people living and fighting in Vietnam in order to find some of the reasons for American failure. This chapter will concentrate on the politicians and people in America in trying to decide why Johnson could not win the war and was eventually forced to retreat. It will look at his confused aims and methods, and changes of mind about them by American officials and people. The chapter will conclude with an account of Johnson's abortive peace moves in his disastrous last months, and an assessment of his actions.

1 Problems with Johnson's Aims and Methods

One of the keys to understanding why Johnson could not defeat the Communists lies in the nature of his aims and methods.

It is not always easy to discover Johnson's aims. Nearly half of Americans polled in 1967 did not know for sure what the war was all about. McNamara's assistant privately quantified American aims as,

> seventy per cent to avoid a humiliating US defeat (to our reputation as a guarantor). Twenty per cent to keep South Vietnamese (and the adjacent) territory from Chinese hands. Ten per cent to permit the people of South Vietnam to enjoy a better, freer way of life.

Johnson publicly said he aimed to defeat Communist aggression, build a nation in South Vietnam and search for peace there. His other aims were best kept private. He wanted to save American face, which he believed necessitated continuing and winning the war. He also wanted to ensure that his conduct of the war did not adversely affect the electoral prospects of any Democrat (especially himself). The problem was that the publicly stated American aims were probably impossible to achieve - certainly with the methods Johnson used and the criticism they aroused.

Johnson's methods included advising, supporting and trying to strengthen the Saigon governments. From 1965 he dramatically increased the numbers of US troops in South Vietnam and changed their role from an advisory to a participatory one. He bombed the

North and the Ho Chi Minh Trail, down which supplies travelled. He hoped this would convince Hanoi that it could not win, and must therefore accept a peace settlement. These methods did not bring an American victory.

The Kennedy and Johnson administrations considered the problem in Vietnam to be the weakness in the Saigon government and in its military performance. They could not see that any 'state' which needed as much support and change as South Vietnam did was simply not viable. Washington talked of bringing democracy to Vietnam but the concept was meaningless to the Vietnamese. There was no Vietnamese tradition of political democracy, no historic development of the belief that the best way to ensure equality was to give all men the vote. That was a belief characteristic of western nations. The strongest Vietnamese political tradition was the hatred of foreigners. What Americans insisted on seeing as a South Vietnamese state went against that most powerful tradition, for the South Vietnamese regimes were all too clearly bound up with and dependent upon the American foreigners. The Vietnamese peasants were often politically apathetic. Their concern was their day-to-day struggle for existence. When a leader offered ideas that might ease that struggle, many were attracted. Ho and the Communists offered another vision of freedom and equality, one characterised by the fairer distribution of wealth. Although Ho was greatly aided by Moscow and Beijing, their help was not as visible as American help in the South. Ho thus combined the appeal of nationalism and equality in a way that the South Vietnamese regimes never managed. The American-sponsored governments in Saigon were generally corrupt, uncaring and unattractive to the ordinary Vietnamese. Thieu told Johnson that the Communists would win any South Vietnamese elections, but Johnson said: 'I don't believe that. Does anyone believe that?'

Johnson never really understood what motivated Ho and his armies. In April 1965 he promised Ho economic aid if he would stop the war: 'Old Ho, can't turn that down.' Johnson did not seem to understand that Ho was fighting for a united Communist Vietnam and would not compromise. Chapter 6 suggested that the North Vietnamese knew why they fought and were willing to wait, suffer and persevere to achieve their aims in a way that many Americans and South Vietnamese were not.

The commander-in-chief bears ultimate responsibility for the choice of weapons and tactics used by his subordinates, but naturally Johnson often deferred to his military experts. 'Bomb, bomb, bomb - that's all they know,' he sighed. Johnson's military men used the wrong methods in Vietnam. They told Johnson they could destroy North Vietnam's industrial and economic base and morale but there were relatively few North Vietnamese factories and roads to destroy. Supplies could come in from China and the USSR. If the Americans bombed one part of the Ho Chi Minh Trail the North Vietnamese could simply change route. The bombing only succeeded in increasing North Vietnamese determination and raising morale, as the CIA pointed out from 1965 onwards. The bombing alienated many Americans and most Vietnamese. From 1962 Agent Orange was used to defoliate 20 per cent of South Vietnam's jungles so that the enemy could be more easily seen, and to kill the rice crops which were partly used for feeding the VC. Bombs and chemicals best suited American technological superiority, wealth and reluctance to lose American lives, but they were not the way to win this war: these methods alienated friendly and neutral Vietnamese and Americans themselves, contributing greatly to American failure in Vietnam. It was not surprising that the Communists controlled most of the countryside, as the JCS admitted in February 1968. In 1995 McNamara wrote that the administration was wrong to allow an arrogant American military to attempt a hi-tech war of attrition against a primarily guerrilla force willing to absorb massive casualties, in a state like South Vietnam which lacked the political stability and popularity necessary to conduct effective military and pacification operations. Westmoreland's emphasis upon 'search and destroy' tactics were inappropriate against guerrillas who could disappear without trace.

The Americans did try to win the hearts and minds of the people with social, medical and educational programmes. Johnson was all too aware of the sufferings of Vietnamese civilians caught in the crossfire and dreamed of bringing prosperity to Vietnam. Inevitably, however, the military emphasis dominated in wartime. 'Grab them by the balls, and their hearts and minds will follow,' said American officers.

Between 1965 and 1968 Johnson's administration slowly became convinced that their aims, methods and vision were inappropriate. It became clear that the escalation of US military involvement in support of the Saigon regime was not going to stop Hanoi and that the involvement was becoming increasingly unpopular amongst Americans and South Vietnamese. Johnson would be forced to retreat because his aims and methods in Vietnam were inappropriate and increasingly unpopular.

2 Why and How Johnson was Forced to Retreat

Even as Johnson was building up American forces in Vietnam in 1965-7, the problems which would eventually defeat him were becoming obvious. The Saigon government remained ineffective and unpopular, and increasing numbers of Americans doubted the wisdom of continuing to support it.

a) Problems in South Vietnam in 1966-7

During 1966-7 Johnson poured more men into Vietnam but the situation there did not look promising. In February 1966 Johnson met Ky in Hawaii. Ky said he wanted a Great Society for Vietnam. 'Boy, you speak just like an American,' said the delighted Johnson. That was not surprising. Ky's speech had been written by his American advisers! Ky's government was in reality corrupt and averse to reform. Ky and his American allies were unpopular. Many South Vietnamese wanted negotiations with Hanoi. There were many protests in Saigon: a Buddhist nun sat cross-legged, her hands clasped in prayer, in a temple in Hue. A friend doused her with gasoline. The nun lit a match to set herself alight while the friend poured peppermint oil on her to disguise the smell of burning flesh. The dead nun's letters were widely circulated; they blamed Johnson for her death because he helped the repressive Saigon regime. 'What are we doing here?' asked one American official when American marines helped Ky attack Buddhist strongholds. 'We are fighting to save these people and they are fighting each other.' At Johnson's insistence Ky held democratic elections. The elections were observed by American politicians and VIPs, one of whom kept calling the country 'South Vietcong'! Although Ky ran the election, his candidate for president, Thieu, still managed only 37 per cent of the vote.

The Johnson administration was publicly optimistic, claiming in 1967 that the 'crossover point' had been reached: American and ARVN troops were killing the enemy faster than they could be replaced. Westmoreland said that there were only 285,000 Communists left fighting in the south (the CIA said over 500,000, but the administration kept it quiet to preserve morale). Privately the administration was pessimistic. Its members disagreed over how the war should be prosecuted. 'Rolling Thunder' was causing tremendous divisions. Johnson railed against 'gutless' officials who leaked 'defeatist' stories to the press: 'It's gotten so you can't have inter-course with your wife without it being spread by traitors.' Things were clearly going badly in Vietnam and it was destroying confidence within the administration. The most worrying loss was Secretary of Defence McNamara.

b) The Loss of McNamara

Johnson had always thought very highly of McNamara. McNamara had been vital in the formulation of Kennedy and Johnson's Vietnam policies but McNamara's Kennedy friends had become passionately anti-war. Bobby Kennedy publicly opposed the war from January 1966. Johnson privately insulted 'nervous Nellies' who disagreed with him about Vietnam, calling one senator a 'prick', Senator Fulbright 'Senator Halfbright', and Bobby Kennedy 'spineless'. Johnson considered the Kennedy-McNamara relationship dangerous.

McNamara's health and family life had suffered because of the war. His daughter and son had told him that what America was doing in Vietnam was immoral and joined in anti-war protests. McNamara blamed himself for his wife's stomach ulcer. He seemed physically and mentally tortured, bursting into tears during discussions. He was losing his old certainty. McNamara told Johnson in early 1967,

> The picture of the world's greatest superpower killing or seriously injuring 1,000 non-combatants a week, while trying to pound a tiny, backward nation into submission on an issue whose merits are hotly disputed, is not a pretty one.

In August 1967 hawks organised Senate hearings designed to force Johnson into lifting restrictions on the bombing of North Vietnam. Public opinion polls in spring 1967 revealed that 45 per cent of Americans favoured increased military pressure in Vietnam (41 per cent favoured withdrawal). During the hearings the military blamed McNamara and Johnson for tying their hands behind their backs, by limiting the bombing. McNamara testified that the bombing was not worth risking a clash with the Soviets. He said bombing would only stop Hanoi if there was sufficient to annihilate North Vietnam and all its people. He pointed out that bombing of the Ho Chi Minh Trail did not stop Communist troops and supplies moving south. Johnson and the JCS were furious with McNamara's performance. The president thought McNamara had degenerated into 'an emotional basket case'. The JCS said his doubts were undermining all the rationale for America's previous and present efforts. Suffering from severe chest pains, McNamara was relieved to move to a job outside the government. In November 1967 in a last tearful White House conference McNamara condemned,

> the goddamned Air Force and its goddamned bombing campaign that had dropped more bombs on Vietnam than on Europe in the whole of World War II and we hadn't gotten a goddamned thing for it.

He had not advocated getting out of Vietnam, only halting the escalation. His administration colleagues considered this unacceptable.

In January 1968 Johnson selected Clark Clifford as Secretary of Defence. In July 1967 he had toured the countries helping the US in Vietnam. In exchange for enormous American aid, South Korea had contributed 45,000 troops; Australia 5,000; Thailand 2,000; the Philippines 2,000 (non-combatants); New Zealand under 500. Clifford told Johnson that 'more people turned out in New Zealand to demonstrate against our trip than the country had sent to Vietnam'. Like his predecessor, Clifford began to doubt the domino theory and the wisdom of US involvement. The Tet offensive finally made Clifford conclude that he had to extricate America from this endless war.

c) The Tet Offensive, January 1968

In January 1968 Hanoi launched an unprecedented offensive against

South Vietnam. Tens of thousands of NVA and VC attacked cities and military installations in the South. 'Uncle Ho was very old and we had to liberate the South before his death,' explained one North Vietnamese officer. Hanoi dreamed that their great offensive would cause the Saigon government to collapse. At the very least Hanoi hoped to demonstrate such strength that America would give up.

The attack broke the traditional Tet holiday truce. The Americans and South Vietnamese were preoccupied with the Tet festival, the Vietnamese equivalent of Christmas, New Year and Easter combined. Saigon, Washington and the US public were shocked that the Communists could move with such impunity and so effectively throughout the South. The American ambassador had to flee the embassy in Saigon in his pyjamas. It took 11,000 American and ARVN troops three weeks to clear Saigon of Communist forces. The attackers had even hit the US embassy and dramatic scenes there were headline news in America. The offensive cost a great many lives and caused incredible damage. 3,895 Americans, 4,954 South Vietnamese military, 14,300 South Vietnamese civilians, and 58,373 VC and NVA died. Out of 17,134 houses in historic Hue, 9,776 were totally destroyed and 3,169 were seriously damaged.

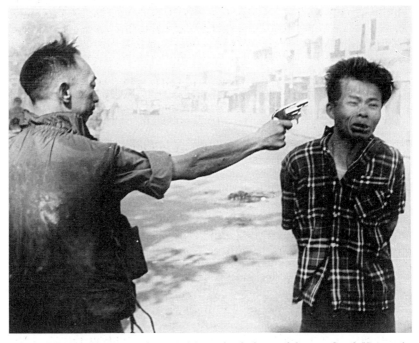

One of the most famous and most misinterpreted photos of the war. South Vietnam's police chief executed a VC in Saigon during the Tet offensive (1968)

The Tet offensive was one of those rare battles lost by both sides. The attackers had suffered grievous losses and ignominy. The unprepared South Vietnamese people had not risen en masse to help them, which damaged the VC claim to be a liberation force. It took Hanoi several years to get over this great effort. Ironically, the impact on the US was equally significant. The ordinary people had not rallied to the Saigon regime. US intelligence officials had failed to notice clear warnings and their confidence was shaken. Had Americans and President Thieu known their Vietnamese history better, they would have remembered that in Tet in 1789 the Vietnamese defeated a Chinese occupation army distracted by the festival. Tet so shook Westmoreland that one American official considered him almost broken. The administration had been claiming that America was winning the war but the TV pictures suggested US failure: even the American embassy was unsafe. One famous photo of a Saigon general shooting a bound captive in the head damaged Americans' faith in their side as the 'good guys'. (Only later was it discovered that the captive was a VC death-squad member who had just shot a relation of the general.) An anti-war newsman repeated an unforgettable and telling soldier's phrase about one South Vietnamese village: 'We had to destroy the town to save it.' That phrase made many Americans question what was being done in Vietnam. US reporters presented a uniformly hostile and negative picture of the Tet offensive, so that Americans felt it was a great defeat. Militarily it was not; psychologically it was. Johnson performed badly at the press conferences following Tet:

> It may be that General Westmoreland makes some serious mistakes or that I make some. We don't know. We are just acting in the light of information we have ... There will be moments of encouragement and discouragement.

Johnson is often criticised for dishonesty but it has to be said that, on occasions such as this, when he was honest he was so uninspiring as to seem guilty of lack of leadership. After Tet his approval ratings plummeted.

At the same time as Tet, the battle of Khe Sanh was being fought. Successfully designed to distract the Americans from the Tet offensive, Khe Sanh was the biggest and bloodiest battle of the war: 10,000 Communists and 500 Americans died. Westmoreland wrongly thought that Khe Sanh was the great prize. This was the kind of fight he wanted, against uniformed and easily identifiable NVA troops. Westmoreland wanted to use tactical nuclear weapons but Washington said no, 'kicked him upstairs' to a desk job and replaced him.

Johnson had a model of Khe Sanh in the Situation Room of the White House, and spent many sleepless nights inspecting it. Clifford feared that the president and indeed the whole government of the United States was on the verge of coming apart. The JCS repeatedly requested more troops. Clifford questioned them about their plan for victory and concluded that they did not have one. By March Clifford was totally against the war and even Rusk was wavering. Back in September 1967 the CIA director had said America could get out of Vietnam without suffering any great loss of international standing. The treasury said the nation could not afford to send more troops and even hawkish senators said 'no more men'. Tet had shaken the confidence of the American government and people. Pictures of destruction and death had turned many Americans against the war.

d) The Collapse of the Home Front

Johnson and Congress naturally paid great attention to public opinion. It is generally agreed that opposition to the war from the public and in the press was probably the main reason why Johnson finally decided upon retreat. However, the objectors were probably a minority, and supporters of the war also put pressure on Johnson. The latter wanted him to continue the fighting. In order to understand both why Johnson continued to wage the war and why he decided to retreat, we need to look at public and press opinion.

Cold Warriors criticised Johnson for not escalating enough. These hawks felt American boys were being forced to fight the Communists with one hand tied behind their backs. They were angry that America never used more than half of its combat-ready divisions and tactical air power in Vietnam. 'Win or get out' was a popular bumper sticker. Many believed American boys, who fought out there on the orders of an elected president and funded by an elected Congress, deserved more support from the folks back home. Those who wonder why Johnson continued to escalate for so long often forget right-wing pressure upon him. On the other hand, not all conservatives approved of the war. Many considered developed areas such as Europe and Japan more important to America. One retired general argued that Asians did not want American ideas 'crammed down their throats'. Many Americans hated the thought of themselves or their loved ones having to fight in Vietnam. Some were repelled by the sufferings of Vietnamese non-combatants. Some Americans felt their international image was suffering. One said that,

> By any objective standard, the United States has become the most aggressive power in the world, the greatest threat to peace, to national self-determination, and to international co-operation.

College students were in the forefront of protest, especially after February 1968 when the draft boards stopped automatic exemption for students. As in all wars many were convicted for violating the draft (952 in 1967). Many draft dodgers (some claim 50,000) slipped into Canada. College students used ingenious methods to avoid the draft: braces on your teeth meant one year's deferment if your teeth were really crooked, and six months if they seemed straight! Young men psyched themselves up to have apparent blood pressure problems when tested, or feigned mental instability. Claiming to have considered suicide usually did the trick. One interesting by-product of the war was a fall in academic standards as colleges swelled with students motivated only by a desire to avoid the war and distracted by protests against it! Some professors were reluctant to fail students who might thereby be drafted.

There are many debates about anti-war protesters on the streets and in the press. To what extent did they affect government policy in Washington and Hanoi? Were protesters just a vocal minority? In order to try to answer these questions we need to look at the chronological history of public opinion through protests, polls and TV.

The protests really began in 1964. 1,000 students from the prestigious Yale University staged a protest march in New York and 5,000 professors wrote in support. However, the Gulf of Tonkin resolution and the presidential election suggest that at this stage Johnson had near unanimous support for his Vietnam policy from the public and most congressmen.

During 1965 many universities held a 'teach-in', with anti-war lectures and debates. 20,000 participated in Berkeley, a leading Californian university. However, thousands of students signed pro-Johnson petitions, including one quarter of Yale undergraduates. Thousands of other citizens participated in protests. In April 25,000 protesters marched on Washington. A young Quaker father of three, holding his baby daughter in his arms, set himself on fire outside McNamara's Pentagon window. There was frequent disorder. 8,000 marchers in Oakland (many from Berkeley) clashed with the police and vandalised cars and buildings. Johnson insisted the protests were financed by Communist governments, and that protesters encouraged the enemy. During 1965, congressional unanimity developed cracks. One congressman reported 'widened unrest' among colleagues in January 1965. As yet, the opposition had little practical impact on American involvement, and 1965 saw the introduction of tens of thousands of additional American ground troops to Vietnam. Naturally, the introduction of American ground troops to the war made a big difference. The increasing number of troops and casualties meant that in 1965 the press and TV networks went to Vietnam in full force. The war became America's first fully televised war. People talked of 'the living-room war' as Americans watched it on every evening news. In August 1965 Johnson was informed that increasing numbers of American reporters in Saigon were 'thoroughly sour and poisonous in their reporting'.

During 1966 public support for the war dropped dramatically. William Fulbright, Chairman of the Senate Foreign Relations Committee, who had steered the Gulf of Tonkin resolution through the Senate, decided that Johnson and McNamara had lied about the second North Vietnamese attack. During Fulbright's February 1966 Foreign Relations Committee hearings on the war, senators spoke against the bombing, and many said Vietnam was not vital to America and withdrawal would do no great harm. The Democratic Party suffered a sharp defeat in the mid-term elections of November 1966 and congressmen blamed Vietnam. They urged Johnson to end the war before it damaged the Great Society and the party. Congress nevertheless continued to fund the war, unwilling to face accusations of betraying American boys in the field. There were relatively few marches and only one state governor refused to declare his support for government policy. However, Johnson felt bound to limit his public appearances to avoid chants of 'Hey, hey, LBJ, how many boys have you killed today?' He was infuriated by noisy demonstrators: 'How can I hit them in the nuts? Tell me how I can hit them in the nuts.'

Westmoreland complained that 'The enemy leaders were made to appear to be the good guys' by the media. Government propaganda was pedestrian and ineffective and (unlike the Second World War) Hollywood gave minimal assistance. Two ageing national institutions did their best. Veteran comedian Bob Hope sought to recapture the camaraderie of the Second World War, giving shows to servicemen in Vietnam. John Wayne made a poor film, *The Green Berets*. The film's idealisation of Americans in Vietnam aroused much hostile criticism but it drew large audiences. This might have reflected the enduring box-office magnetism of its star, the appeal of war films, the undiscriminating movie-going habits of the masses, support for the war from the 'silent majority', or a combination of all these factors.

As yet, the criticism had not caused Johnson to alter his policies, but during 1967 opposition to the war grew. Tens of thousands protested in the great cities of America. Congressmen put ever more pressure on Johnson. The churches and black civil rights leader Martin Luther King led the opposition. Black people resented the disproportionate number of black casualties in Vietnam and felt kinship with the poor, non-white Vietnamese. When King saw a picture of Vietnamese children showing burn wounds from American napalm bombs in January 1967 he became publicly critical. He said the poverty programme had raised hope for the inhabitants of the inner-city ghettos, but now the funds were being diverted to the war. Young black males, 'crippled by their own society', were being sent to

1 guarantee liberties in Southeast Asia which they had not found in Southwest Georgia and east Harlem ... We have been repeatedly faced with the cruel irony of watching Negro and white boys on TV screens as they kill and die together for a nation that has been unable to seat
5 them together in the same schools. I could never again raise my voice against the violence of the oppressed in the ghettos without having first spoken clearly to the greatest purveyor of violence in the world today - my own government.

Tax rises turned more Americans against the war in August 1967. In October 1967 draft cards were publicly burned throughout the country. Berkeley radicals tried to close down the draft headquarters in Oakland. The police attacked 2,500 demonstrators with clubs and the demonstrators retaliated with cans, bottles and smoke bombs. The demonstrators put thousands of ball bearings on the street to stop police on horseback. 4,000-10,000 demonstrators brought the streets around the draft headquarters to a standstill. They escaped from 2,000 police officers, then vandalised cars, parking meters, newsstands and trees. Many were high on drugs. The divisions between liberal and radical protesters were well illustrated in a Washington rally. Johnson had 2,000 policemen, 17,000 National Guard troops and 6,000 regular army men to meet 70,000 protesters. Most of the protesters just listened to speeches but some radicals were involved in violence outside the Pentagon. McNamara watched from his office window and found it 'terrifying. Christ, yes, I was scared.' The government's bill for the operations was just over $1 million. There were 625 arrests.

Abe Fortas believed that McNamara was one who had been over-influenced by the protesters. In some ways Fortas had a good point. During August 1967 hawkish senators had conducted hearings aimed at pressurising Johnson into lifting all restrictions on bombing in Vietnam. The respected and experienced group of elder statesmen nicknamed the 'Wise Men' and including Acheson and Rusk, all assured Johnson that they supported his Vietnam policy. Such support for the war and escalation is too often forgotten because it is overshadowed by the drama of the protests. On the other hand, a growing number of Johnson's friends and supporters were changing their views on the war because the loss of someone close to them, or because their children opposed the war. Those in the White House were increasingly unsettled. McNamara left and Dean Rusk's son disagreed so intensely with his father over Vietnam that his psychiatrist told him, 'You had your father's nervous breakdown [for him].' In 1966 Rusk had visited an army hospital in Saigon where a nurse,

> stared long and hard at me with a look of undisguised hatred ... from the look on her face she clearly held me responsible for what had happened to those men. I never forgot the look on that nurse's face.

Pinpointing turning points in support for the war is difficult, but it seems that 1967 was crucial. Some influential newspapers and TV stations shifted from support to opposition. Draft calls, deaths in Vietnam and taxes all increased, arousing more discontent, but it is difficult to know exactly how many opposed Johnson's policies. Polls can be misleading. In October 1967 46 per cent of Americans felt the Vietnam commitment was a mistake, yet a massive majority wanted to stay there and get tougher - so, one could say that this poll indicated both widespread support and widespread opposition to the war. 'I want to get out but I don't want to give up', said one housewife to a pollster. Even the White House was surprised by a poll which showed considerable support for the war in early 1968: 49 per cent to 29 per cent favoured invading North Vietnam and 42 per cent to 33 per cent favoured mining Haiphong (the main port in North Vietnam) even if Soviet ships were sunk as a result; 25 per cent did not oppose bombing China or using atomic weapons. There were nearly half a million Americans in Vietnam and nearly 17,000 had died there but Johnson's policies still had considerable support.

Perhaps the media coverage of the Tet offensive in early 1968 was the crucial turning point. Walter Cronkite, the most respected TV journalist, had been strongly supportive of the war until a February 1968 visit to Vietnam. He concluded the war could not be won. Some saw his defection as a great turning point: in the next few weeks Johnson's approval rating fell from 48 per cent to 36 per cent. The Communists might have been defeated militarily, but Tet suggested Johnson was losing the battle for the hearts and minds of an important percentage of his people. Some were against the war altogether, others wanted him to wage it differently. A minority were protesting vociferously.

It is difficult to trace the interrelationship between the protests and rising dissatisfaction in Congress and in the White House itself, but there is no doubt that politicians were sensitive to the wishes of the voters and the protesters probably played a part disproportionate to their numbers in bringing the war toward an end. By the spring of 1968, Johnson had lost confidence if not in the rectitude of his policies then at least in his capacity to maintain continued support for them. The protesters and the media had suggested his war and his way of conducting it were wrong and this played an important part in loss of confidence amongst White House officials and the troops in Vietnam.

e) Financial and Economic Problems

The war cost a great deal of money and distorted the economy. Johnson did not want to admit how much he was spending lest conservatives in Congress cut off payments for his Great Society programmes, so he was slow to ask for the necessary wartime tax rises. In 1965 the government deficit had been $1.6 billion. By 1968 it was $25.3 billion. Such deficits caused inflation and endangered America's economic well-being. The Treasury warned him that this should not go on and tax payers grew resentful, increasing the pressure on him to change direction in Vietnam.

f) Johnson's Loss of Confidence

Not surprisingly by the spring of 1968 Johnson was losing confidence. He frequently grabbed visitors to the White House, thrust his face into theirs and cried out, 'What would you do?' about Vietnam. Johnson described how 'I lay awake picturing my boys flying around North Vietnam' bombing the targets he had picked for them. 'Suppose one of my boys misses his mark … [and] one of his bombs falls on one of those Russian ships in the harbour?' Johnson imagined he saw an American plane shot down: 'I saw it hit the ground, and as soon as it burst into flames, I couldn't stand it any more. I knew that one of my boys must have been killed.' He received conflicting advice, as he told his brother Sam in February:

1   That's just the trouble … it's always my move. And, damn it, I sometimes can't tell whether I'm making the right move or not. Now take this Vietnam mess. How in the hell can anyone know for sure what's right and what's wrong, Sam? I got some of the finest brains in this country -
5   people like Dean Rusk … and Dean Acheson - making some strong convincing arguments for us to stay in there and not pull out. Then I've got some people like George Ball and Fulbright - also intelligent men whose motives I can't rightly distrust - who keep telling me we've got to de-escalate or run the risk of a total war. And, Sam, I've got to listen
10 to both sides … I've just got to choose between my opposing experts … But I sure as hell wish I could REALLY know what's right.

Johnson's health was suffering. In her diary Lady Bird described 10 March as a 'day of deep gloom'. 14 March was 'one of those terrific, pummelling White House days that can stretch and grind and use you'. Her husband was 'bone weary', 'dead tired', and unable to sleep. 'Those sties are coming back on Lyndon's eyes. First one and then the other, red and swollen and painful.' On 31 March, 'his face was sagging and there was such pain in his eyes as I had not seen since his mother died'.

On 25 March 1968 the 'Wise Men' met. They were changing their minds. Now most advocated some kind of retreat in Vietnam. Johnson could not believe that 'these establishment bastards have bailed out'. Congress was pressing hard for retreat, and the polls were discouraging. 78 per cent of Americans believed America was not making any progress in the war, 74 per cent that Johnson was not handling it well. The war-induced balance of payments deficit had dramatically weakened the dollar on the international money market, causing a gold crisis which was the final straw for many Americans. From now on Johnson knew there would have to be some sort of a reversal in Vietnam.

Johnson agonised over how to announce any change in US policy, unwilling to admit his country had been in error and unwilling to betray those Americans who were fighting and dying in Vietnam. On 31 March 1968 he offered to stop bombing North Vietnam if Hanoi would agree to talks and said he would not be running for re-election. Some think Johnson's decision not to run was a reaction to the unpopularity of his Vietnam policies but both he and Lady Bird were genuinely anxious about his poor health. He claimed that

> I've given up the presidency, given up politics, to search for peace. No
> one worries more about this war than I do. It's broken my heart - in a
> way, broken my back. But I think I can get these people at the confer-
> ence table.

3 Johnson's Last Months

a) Peace Talks

Peace talks had been a recurring theme throughout Johnson's presidency. One of his great aims in escalation and particularly Rolling
Thunder had been to 'persuade' Hanoi it could not win and therefore should negotiate. Ho however rejected negotiations as long as
the bombing continued, while Johnson said the bombing would only
stop when Hanoi stopped waging war in the South. To show willing,
Johnson ordered several bombing pauses, but he hated them. 'Oh
yes, a bombing halt,' he would say, 'I'll tell you what happens when
there's a bombing halt: I halt and then Ho Chi Minh shoves trucks up
my ass.' There were attempts at negotiation, usually by foreign inter-
mediaries such as Poland in 1966 (this failed when Johnson ordered
that Hanoi be bombed more heavily than usual) and Britain in 1967.
Britain concluded that Washington was never serious about these
peace initiatives. Senator Fulbright agreed:

> All you guys are committed to a military settlement. You don't want to
> negotiate; you're not going to negotiate. You are bombing that little piss-
> ant country up there, and you think you can blow them up. It's a bunch
> of crap about wanting to negotiate.

With Johnson's loss of confidence by spring 1968, the prospects
improved. Hanoi was exhausted after Tet, anxious to divide
Americans, and keen to negotiate. Talks began at Paris in May 1968.
America demanded a North Vietnamese withdrawal from South
Vietnam and rejected Communist participation in the Saigon govern-
ment, while North Vietnam demanded American withdrawal from
South Vietnam and insisted on VC participation in the Saigon govern-
ment. No wonder the talks continued intermittently for five years!
Johnson recognised the need for some sort of retreat but was not the
man to do it: he just could not bring himself to accept Hanoi's terms.

> 1 If I left that war and let the Communists take over South Vietnam, then
>   I would be seen as a coward and my nation would be seen as an
>   appeaser, and we would both find it impossible to accomplish anything
>   for anybody anywhere in the entire globe ... Nothing was worse than
> 5 that.

b) The Disintegration of Johnson's Presidency

Events in the last few months of Johnson's presidency confirmed the need for a dramatic change in America's Vietnam policy. The fighting had reached maximum intensity in the first half of 1968. In two weeks in May alone, 1,800 Americans were killed and 18,000 seriously wounded. US forces, now numbering over half a million, had began to suffer the severe morale problems that would soon lead to virtual collapse.

The Democratic Party convention was held in Chicago in August 1968. Thousands of anti-war protesters turned out. Leading hippies calling themselves the Yippies (Youth International Party) nominated a live pig called Pigasus for president. A youth lowered the American flag and was beaten and arrested by police. With cries of 'Pigs!' the crowd threw stones and cans at the tense and combative police, who hit back with batons and tear gas, then began indiscriminate attacks on people. There were 668 arrests and 192 police injuries. Continuation of the war seemed to be leading to the disintegration of American society.

On 31 October 1968 Johnson ordered the cessation of the bombing of North Vietnam, partly, if not predominantly, to help ensure that Vice-President Humphrey won the 1968 presidential election. However, the negotiations with Hanoi stalled. Despite many suggestions for the number and shape of tables, the negotiators could not even agree on where to sit: Thieu, for example, refused to sit at the same table as Hanoi. The battle of the tables was the last battle of Johnson's administration.

Humphrey lost the election, partly because of his inability to dissociate himself sufficiently from Johnson's Vietnam policy. However, like polls, elections are notorious for not telling the whole story. When the Democratic peace candidate Senator Eugene McCarthy did so well against Johnson in the New Hampshire primary, it emerged that hawks greatly outnumbered doves amongst McCarthy 'supporters', which shows the difficulty of interpreting votes. McCarthy's 'victory' was seen as a vote for peace, when it could more accurately be seen as a vote to force Johnson to escalate. The Republican candidate Richard Nixon pledged to bring an honourable end to the war in Vietnam, but a vote for him was not necessarily a vote against the war. Some voted according to habit or on domestic issues. The third candidate, the renegade Democrat George Wallace, was a pro-war candidate and he picked up many votes. It is therefore difficult to ascertain the role and unpopularity of the Vietnam war in the result. All we can conclude is that in 1968 the voters remained divided over Vietnam. Johnson's presidency and war effort had disintegrated primarily because of these American divisions.

4 Conclusions About Johnson and the War

Why had Johnson failed to win the war? The bottom line was that the establishment of a viable South Vietnamese state was beyond the powers of Johnson's America. Johnson considered real escalation an impossibility: it might bring the Soviets and Chinese in, and attacking 'little' North Vietnam would damage America's international image. So America just continued to fight a limited and ineffective war to support a series of unpopular Saigon regimes. The nature of the warfare and criticism back home led to the apparent collapse of the home front and the American forces in Vietnam.

Had Johnson's Vietnam policy been a total failure? He had restrained American hawks, whose policies might have led to full-scale war with China or the USSR. Perhaps Communist insurgents in other parts of Southeast Asia did badly in the 1960s because American actions in Vietnam encouraged anti-Communists and kept China busy.

Why did Johnson not get out? Hanoi was not going to give up, so neutralisation or peace would mean a coalition government containing Communists, which was unacceptable to Johnson and many other Americans. Johnson thought getting out of Vietnam on those terms would damage the credibility of himself, his party and his country and be a betrayal of the Americans who had fought and died there.

What had the war done to America? We have seen that the war damaged America's armed forces, image, morale, national unity and economy. It also damaged the presidency and American society.

How did Johnson and the Vietnam war damage the presidency? During 1965 the media became increasingly hostile, partly because of the Vietnam policies, partly because of Johnson and McNamara's lack of straightforwardness in describing them. When the marines landed in Danang in March 1965, the State Department readily admitted it, to Johnson's fury. He said there had been 'no change', which was untrue. The 'credibility gap' was the difference between what Johnson said and what actually was. One wit said that Johnson lost the most important battle of the Vietnam war, the 'Battle of Credibility Gap'! It had an adverse impact on the presidency; respect for the office decreased because of the increasingly unpopular and apparently dishonest person who held it.

How did the war damage American society? 'Vietnam took it all away,' said Kennedy's brother-in-law, Sargent Shriver, 'every god-damned dollar. That's what killed the war on poverty.' Between 1965 and 1973 $15.5 billion was spent on the Great Society, compared to $120 billion on the war in Vietnam. During Johnson's presidency 222,351 US military were killed or wounded in Vietnam. Returning American veterans had physical and/or mental disabilities that for the most part would remain with them for the rest of their lives. Many veterans returned with drug problems and with sharpened class and racial antagonisms. Ethnic minorities and poor whites knew that middle-class white males were under-represented in Vietnam, except in the officer class which they dominated. The middle class had frequently used their money and intelligence to avoid combat whether by continuing education or convincing the draft board of their uselessness. The unpopularity of the war divided friends and families. Many of these social wounds and divisions remain. A Johnson aide said the war was like a fungus or a contagion: it infected everything it touched and seemed to touch everything. He was right.

As Johnson left the presidency he admitted he had made mistakes. He said history would judge him after current passions had subsided. The passions have still not subsided, for the impact of the war remains with Americans. Johnson is still greatly blamed and frequently reviled.

Summary Diagram
'Johnson's Failure'

Johnson's aim - was it realistic?	Independent, non-Communist South Vietnam

Johnson's methods - were they wise?	Advised / supported Saigon
	US troops
	Bombed

Why did Johnson fail?	Hanoi and VC	Saigon and ARVN	Bombs
	HOME FRONT		

What were the results of Johnson's policies?	Failed to defeat Communists
	Damaged America

Making notes on 'Johnson's Failure'

Examiners frequently ask why America lost the war. Your notes from Chapters 6 and 7 should therefore be detailed and it is important to remember that the two sets of notes cover the same theme. Your Chapter 6 notes concentrated on what was happening in Vietnam, and your Chapter 7 notes will concentrate on what happened in America - together, they will summarise why America was unable to defeat the Communists. Once again a list of 'reasons why' will be your main target. Your list will cover i) why Johnson's aims and methods were doomed to failure, ii) the weakness of America's Saigon ally, iii) the loss of support in America, iv) Tet and v) Johnson's loss of confidence. If you have time, it would be helpful to do parallel date lists of what was happening in i) Vietnam itself, ii) the White House, iii) Congress, iv) the press, and v) amongst ordinary Americans. This will enable you to see the interrelationship between the factors which ensured America's defeat.

Answering essay questions on Chapters 6 and 7 - Why the Americans were unable to defeat the Communists

America's failure is a massive topic which lends itself to a structured essay or a single-statement essay. The following examples are in order of difficulty.

1. **a)** What were the advantages of guerrilla warfare to the Vietnamese Communists? (3 marks)
    b) What were the problems of the Saigon government and ARVN? (4 marks)
    c) In what ways was the American military performance in Vietnam ineffective? (8 marks)
    d) How did the 'home front' contribute to America's inability to defeat the Communists in Vietnam? (10 marks)
[This first question gives you a reasonable essay plan for question 3]
2. **a)** In what ways were the Vietnamese Communists difficult to defeat? (10 marks)
    b) In what ways were the Americans particularly ill-suited to defeating them? (10 marks)
3. Why was Johnson unable to defeat the Vietnamese Communists?
4. 'America was unable to defeat the Vietnamese Communists because of the collapse of the home front.' Do you agree?

Those 4 essay questions basically ask the same question - why America lost. The trick in answering them is to adjust the same series of points (made in Chapters 6 and 7) to the specific requirements of each question. In answering question 4 it might be tempting to spend the whole essay on the home front, but it is best to utilise all your standard paragraphs on 'Why America failed', weighing up the role (if any) and relative importance of the home front within each paragraph. For example, in your 'problems with Saigon' paragraph, you could say that Americans back home disliked Thieu's undemocratic government, and that this helped increase domestic American opposition to the war. Naturally, your 'home front' section will be longer than the others as question 4 concentrates upon it.

Source-based questions on 'Johnson's Failure'

1. The American Retreat from Vietnam

Look at the extracts from McNamara (page 97), Johnson's press conference (page 99), the commentator on page 100, Martin Luther King (page 102), Rusk (page 103), and Johnson talking to his brother (page 105). Answer these questions.

a) Who were: (i) Rusk; (ii) Acheson; and (iii) Fulbright? (3 marks)

b) Judging from the sources, in what ways was world opinion anti-American during the Vietnam war? (3 marks)

c) In what ways and to what extent do the tone and style make Martin Luther King's speech an effective anti-war statement? (5 marks)

d) What are the strengths and weaknesses of Johnson's conversation with his brother Sam as evidence for the historian seeking to understand Johnson's decision-making processes? (6 marks)

e) Using these sources and your background knowledge, explain why many Americans had decided by 1968 that it was time for an American retreat in Vietnam. (8 marks)

8 1969-73: Richard Nixon, Diplomatic Genius or Mad Bomber?

American involvement in Vietnam finally ended under President Richard Nixon. Historians debate several issues concerning Nixon and Vietnam. Why was it Nixon, the great Cold Warrior and supporter of escalation, who ended the war? Having decided from the outset of his presidency that the war had to be ended, why did Nixon take so long to do so? Did he delay peace until the eve of the 1972 presidential election in order to get re-elected? Why did he apparently escalate the war by bombing Cambodia? These questions will be investigated in this chapter, along with another bigger question facing any student of Nixon. Was he, as some Americans believe, an evil man whose policies were characterised by 'secrecy, duplicity, and a ruthless attention to immediate political advantage regardless of larger moral issues' as the historian Marilyn Young writing in 1991 considered?

1 The Transformation of a Cold Warrior?

Nixon first made his name as a politician because of his extreme anti-Communism. He championed crusades against Communists at home and abroad, yet got America out of Vietnam and drew closer to the Soviets and Chinese than any previous Cold War president. How did this happen? Was there a genuine conversion or 'ruthless attention to immediate political advantage'? After years of being the leading Republican Cold Warrior, a combination of events made Nixon change his traditional stance.

a) Vice-President and Cold Warrior

During his years as Eisenhower's vice-president (1953-61), Nixon had an exceptional apprenticeship in foreign affairs. He frequently travelled abroad and met leaders of many nations. He was present during the foreign policy debates within the Eisenhower administration and had a thorough education in the problem of Vietnam. His ideas differed from Eisenhower's. He wanted to help the French at Dien Bien Phu with an American air strike and was even willing to use (small) atomic bombs. He said that if sending American boys to fight in Vietnam was the only way to stop Communist expansion in Indochina, then the Government should take the 'politically unpopular position' and do it.

b) Republican Foreign Policy Expert

After Kennedy defeated Nixon in the 1960 presidential race, Nixon held no political office for eight years but kept himself in the political news by foreign policy pronouncements.

Like Johnson, he felt:

> Victory [in Vietnam] is essential to the survival of freedom. We have an unparalleled opportunity to roll back the Communist tide, not only in South Vietnam but in Southeast Asia generally and indeed the world as a whole.

As the recognised leader of the Republican opposition on foreign policy, Nixon spurred Johnson to greater involvement in Vietnam. Whatever Johnson did, Nixon urged him to do more. He approved the sending of American ground troops, while wishing for more. 'The United States cannot afford another defeat in Asia,' he said. Nixon called for victory and nothing less. By victory he meant a Korean-style settlement: like Johnson, he wanted two independent Vietnamese states, one of which was not Communist.

Nixon aimed at being the 1968 Republican presidential candidate from 1964 onwards. Naturally he accused the Democrat Johnson of getting everything wrong. He said Johnson had got bogged down in a long, costly ground war. He criticised Johnson for lacking new ideas, but had none himself. He could only advocate more bombing. 'When [President] Nixon said, in 1969, that he had inherited a war not of his making, he was being too modest,' said his biographer Stephen Ambrose.

c) Republican Presidential Candidate

In 1967, presidential hopeful Nixon seemed the last man likely to advocate withdrawal from Vietnam. He criticised the anti-war protesters as a traitorous minority. 'The last desperate hope of North Vietnam is that they can win politically in the United States what our fighting men are denying them militarily in Vietnam.'

In early 1968 Nixon was as shocked as everyone else by Tet. This was a great turning point for him. He realised that there would have to be changes in American policy. He started to call for the increased use of South Vietnamese soldiers, a policy which would soon become known as Vietnamisation:

> The nation's objective should be to help the South Vietnamese fight the war and not fight it for them. If they do not assume the majority of the burden in their own defence, they cannot be saved.

(Kennedy and Johnson had of course said the same but Johnson had nevertheless assumed the 'majority of the burden'.) Nixon said American forces should be withdrawn while the ARVN was built up.

He stopped talking about escalation. There was no more talk of a 'victorious peace' only an 'honourable peace'. 'I pledge to you, new leadership will end the war and win the peace in the Pacific.' Did Nixon really believe that Thieu could maintain a strong South Vietnam without the ever increasing American aid that Nixon had so strongly advocated until Tet? Or was he guilty of 'duplicity?' He probably genuinely believed that Thieu could survive with the help of a change of emphasis in American aid (more American bombing and fewer American soldiers) and a radical change of diplomatic direction. He said America needed to diversify its methods in Vietnam, for example, by using diplomatic leverage with the USSR. The old Cold Warrior emphasised that world Communism had changed. Communism was no longer monolithic, therefore the next president should replace the era of confrontation with the era of negotiation.

The last months of Johnson's presidency were dominated by the Paris peace talks. Doves said a bombing halt would lead Hanoi to negotiate a coalition government in Saigon. Hawks rejected that as nonsense: 'If you give them [Communists] the bombing pause and a coalition government, you give them the whole goddam country,' Nixon said. Nixon's 'peace with honour' necessitated the continuation of Thieu's Saigon regime. In October 1968 there was the possibility of a breakthrough in the Paris peace talks. Hanoi seemed to be offering Thieu an opportunity to remain in power with a coalition government. Nixon disliked the idea of a coalition and also feared that successful talks would jeopardise his chance of beating Hubert Humphrey, the Democratic presidential candidate. 'We don't want to play politics with peace,' said Nixon, but, he subsequently admitted, 'that was inevitably what was happening'. Privately, Nixon encouraged Thieu not to go to Paris. Had Nixon thereby sabotaged the talks? Thieu probably would not have gone anyway. He had nothing to gain there. Thieu totally rejected the idea of a coalition containing Communists and so did Nixon.

d) Had the Cold Warrior Changed?

Had the old Cold Warrior undergone something of a transformation on the eve of his victory in the presidential election? There had been no transformation of Richard Nixon, the political opportunist: he had tried to ensure that it was not Johnson who won 'peace with honour' in Vietnam! Tet had proved conclusively to him that the Vietnam war was not going well, so he decided that America needed to withdraw as soon as possible, leaving South Vietnam to fight and win its own battle. Peace with honour required Thieu to be left in power, in a strong position. There had thus been no transformation of his ultimate aim for South Vietnam, which was that it should survive as an independent state like South Korea. The transformation was tactical. He now advocated Vietnamisation and an improvement in relations with the USSR and China in order to gain peace with honour. The Sino-Soviet split had shattered the threat of a monolithic world Communist bloc. Nixon had decided that America could play off the two rival Communist giants against each other, by improving relations with both. The Cold War world had changed, so thoughtful Cold Warriors had to adapt. Both China and the USSR would be vital in pressing Hanoi to a 'peace with honour' settlement in Vietnam. The political and dramatic impact of being a world peacemaker appealed to Nixon: foreign policy success could help his re-election in 1972. Improved relations with China and the USSR and peace in Vietnam would reinvigorate America and ensure Nixon's place in the history books. An intelligent pragmatism, political ambition, and an element of idealism made the old Cold Warrior ready to end the Vietnam war.

2 President Nixon

a) The President and his Adviser

Nixon thought that foreign policy was the most important and interesting task of any president, and his National Security Adviser, Henry Kissinger, agreed with him.

A Jewish refugee from Nazi Germany, Kissinger arrived in America as a teenager. He became a Harvard professor. He specialised in international relations and, like Nixon, travelled widely and learned fast. Kissinger was politically ambitious. He had tried but failed to attach himself to the Kennedy set. During the presidential election campaign of 1968 he offered his services to several candidates. Until late 1968, Kissinger despised Nixon, 'the most dangerous' of the presidential candidates. He considered Nixon an anti-Communist fanatic, yet offered him information on Democratic election strategy. His desire for power caused him to compromise. Once in the Nixon administration, he liked to pretend he was an innocent academic in the vicious political jungle. If so, he learned fast. 'Henry, you don't remember your old friends,' said a minor civil servant whom he ignored. 'The secret of my success,' said Kissinger, 'is to forget my old friends.' He told a journalist that, 'What interests me is what you can do with power.' He enjoyed the company of glamorous Hollywood actresses, declaring that 'power is the ultimate aphrodisiac'. Kissinger was a great believer in personal and secret diplomacy. He distrusted bureaucrats and, it was commonly said in Washington, treated his staff as mushrooms: kept in the dark, stepped on, and frequently covered with manure. He felt that foreign policy for the most part was 'too complex' for 'the ordinary guy' to understand. Nixon shared those sentiments. This conviction proved to be a problem and a weakness. They did not always explain their diplomacy, and therefore did not always ensure popular support for their policies. Both thought in terms of American national interest with little apparent regard for moral considerations. That *realpolitik* can still arouse shock. Neither seemed to worry as Johnson had about the deaths of Vietnamese civilians or even of American soldiers. Kissinger's contempt for conscientious objectors led him to declare, 'Conscientious objection must be reserved only for the greatest moral issues, and Vietnam is not of this magnitude.' Both Kissinger and Nixon had a brilliant grasp of foreign affairs and favoured by-passing the traditional diplomatic machinery. Nixon chose his old friend and supporter William Rogers to be Secretary of State. Rogers knew little about foreign policy but Nixon told Kissinger this was an advantage as it would ensure White House control! When Rogers got his first pile of foreign policy papers to read, he was amazed. 'You don't expect me to read all this stuff, do you?' The Rogers and Kissinger relationship was tempestuous. Kisssinger repeatedly stormed into Nixon's office threatening resignation unless Rogers was restrained or replaced. Nixon said,

> I'm sorry about how Henry and Bill get at each other. It's really deep-seated. Henry thinks Bill isn't very deep, and Bill thinks Henry is power-crazy. And in a sense, they are both right.

He put it all down to their egos and inferiority complexes! Years later he wrote that:

> Rogers felt that Kissinger was Machiavellian, deceitful, egotistical, arrogant, and insulting. Kissinger felt that Rogers was vain, uninformed, unable to keep a secret, and hopelessly dominated by the State Department bureaucracy.

Nixon and Kissinger spent a great deal of time together and as Nixon's presidency wore on, Kissinger became ever more influential. Unlike Nixon, Kissinger was always treated with the utmost respect by the media. Such was Kissinger's power that on the occasions when he subverted Nixon's intentions, he got away with it. Led by two such hard-headed realists, American foreign policy became what many people would consider careless of 'larger moral issues' in its emphasis upon the ultimate survival and strength of American power. Nixon himself recognised that it would be called 'Machiavellian'.

b) Vietnam: the Problems and Solutions

Upon learning of Johnson's bugging and wiretapping in the White House, Nixon said privately, 'I don't blame him. He's been under such pressure because of that damn war, he'd do anything. I'm not going to end up like LBJ ... I'm going to stop that war. Fast!' Ironically, although Nixon did stop the war, it ruined his presidency too.

Vietnam was Nixon's greatest single problem. His aim was clear: peace. What sort of peace? Peace through a great victory? No. Nixon could not invade North Vietnam nor destroy the NVA. Peace through a straightforward American withdrawal? No. Honour required that

Thieu remain in power. Nixon hoped for a Korean-style settlement, an armistice under which two separate states would coexist. How could he get it? He knew that in 1953 Eisenhower had obtained the Korean armistice through pressure on the USSR and China. Nixon would tempt the Soviets with promises of arms agreements and trade and the Chinese with a normalisation of relations. He also had another ploy:

1 I call it the 'Madman Theory' ... I want the North Vietnamese to believe ... I might do *anything* ... We'll just slip the word to them that, 'for God's sake, you know Nixon is obsessed about Communism. We can't restrain him when he's angry - and he has his hand on the nuclear button' - and
5 Ho Chi Minh himself will be in Paris in two days begging for peace.

In his inaugural address, Nixon said, 'The greatest honour history can bestow is the title of peacemaker.' That America was at war at home as well as abroad was demonstrated in his presidential inaugural parade. Thousands of anti-war demonstrators chanted 'Ho, Ho, Ho Chi Minh, the NLF [the political arm of the VC] is going to win.' Demonstrators burned small American flags and spat at police. Nixon thus had two great tasks as president in 1969. He had to bring peace to America and Vietnam.

3 Why Did Nixon Take So Long To End The War?

Although Nixon was determined to end the war, he had to have his 'peace with honour'. It took time and tremendous effort to persuade Hanoi to agree to allow Thieu to remain in power. Nixon had to use great military and diplomatic pressure to gain a settlement wherein Thieu was given a reasonable chance for survival, and whereby it could not be said that American had wasted its time and effort in Vietnam. Whilst applying the military and diplomatic pressure, Nixon had also to take into account American left-wing opposition to the war, and right-wing opposition to losing it.

a) Military Pressure, 1969-71

In February 1969 the Communists launched another offensive on South Vietnam. Rolling Thunder and the American ground offensive of 1966-8 had clearly not worked, so Nixon decided to try an offensive against the Ho Chi Minh Trail in Cambodia. Nixon hoped this would sever enemy supply lines and encourage Hanoi to agree to an acceptable peace. He also hoped to destroy the supposed Vietnamese Communist headquarters in Cambodia - COSVN (the Central Office for South Vietnam). In March Nixon secretly ordered the bombing of the Cambodian sanctuaries. The bombing failed to destroy COSVN or slow traffic on the trail, so in late April Nixon escalated it. 'I can't believe,' said the exasperated Kissinger, 'that a fourth-rate power like North Vietnam does not have a breaking point.' He advocated blockading Haiphong and invading North Vietnam. Nixon feared domestic opposition to this but deliberately leaked to the press that he was considering it. This was his 'madman' tactic. By the summer Hanoi seemed to be slowing down the fighting.

Nixon thus attempted three solutions to the military problem in 1969: bombing the trail in Cambodia, the 'madman' ploy and Vietnamisation. All were designed to gain peace with honour.

In spring 1970, having announced the withdrawal of 150,000 American troops from Southeast Asia, Nixon nevertheless appeared to be extending the war to Laos and Cambodia. He was apparently escalating again. Why?

Nixon believed that demonstrations of American power would counter Saigon's pessimism about American troop withdrawals, help protect the remaining Americans in Vietnam, intimidate Hanoi and gain better peace terms. He therefore escalated the air offensive in January 1970, heavily bombing the trail in Laos and Cambodia, and North Vietnamese anti-aircraft bases. Nevertheless on 12 February the North Vietnamese launched another great offensive in Laos. Nixon desperately needed to do something effective soon in order to get an acceptable peace, especially as Congress was considering cutting off his money. 30,000 American and ARVN forces therefore moved into south-western Cambodia (less than 50 miles from Saigon) but encountered neither enemy resistance nor COSVN. The Vietnamese had just disappeared. Pressure from American anti-war protesters now forced Nixon to make a speedy withdrawal from Cambodia.

What had Nixon's Cambodian offensive achieved? The capture and destruction of vast quantities of Communist materials meant it was nearly two years before Hanoi launched another major offensive in South Vietnam, which theoretically gave the ARVN time to grow stronger. Nixon claimed that intervention in Cambodia had occupied NVA troops who would otherwise have been killing Americans. However, COSVN had not been found. Perhaps it had never existed. The Americans had expected to find a miniature Pentagon but there were just a few huts. 344 Americans and 818 ARVN died in Cambodia. 1592 Americans and 3,553 ARVN were wounded. Nixon's critics said it had widened the war. The *New York Times* queried whether the offensive had won time for America or just boosted Hanoi by revealing American divisions and the restraints on the president.

By 1971 the morale of the American army in Vietnam had plummeted. This is not surprising. Eighteen-year-olds were still being asked to fight a war that everyone in America agreed was just about finished, in order to allow time for the army of a corrupt dictatorship in Saigon to improve. Nixon warned the West Point graduating class that it was no secret that they would be leading troops guilty of drug abuse and insubordination.

Determined not to be the first president to lose a war and desperate to gain peace with honour, Nixon decided to go on the military offensive again. The JCS had long been tempted by the trail in southern Laos, but Westmoreland thought that would require four American divisions. From late 1970, the JCS argued that the ARVN could do it if protected by American air power. In Cambodia in 1970 the NVA had slipped away to avoid meeting the Americans, but the JCS thought the NVA could be enticed out if it was to meet the ARVN. American bombing could then destroy them. That should help ARVN morale, show Vietnamisation was working, cut the trail, and damage Hanoi's ability to stage an offensive in 1971. Nixon gave the go-ahead. 5,000 ARVN elite troops would go into Laos. Rogers warned that Hanoi expected it (there had been leaks in Saigon), and that Nixon was sending only one ARVN division to do a job Westmoreland would not do without four American divisions. Why get involved in Laos for that? It would damage ARVN morale. Nixon and Kissinger ignored him. The Lam Son offensive began on 8 February 1971. Initially the ARVN did well but then the NVA got the upper hand, thanks especially to new armoured units using Soviet equipment. Within two weeks, the ARVN was routed. Half the force died. American TV viewers saw ARVN troops fighting each other for places on American helicopters lifting them out of Laos. American crews coated the skids with grease so the South Vietnamese would stop hanging on in numbers sufficient to bring down the choppers. After three years of offensives and Vietnamisation, Nixon did not seem to have made any progress on the military front.

b) Diplomatic Pressure

Nixon hoped that if he applied both military and diplomatic pressure in the correct proportions, he would gain 'peace with honour'.

On the diplomatic front, Nixon's first initiative was the April 1969 suggestion that, as the Paris peace talks had stalled amidst the public posturing, there should be secret Washington-Hanoi negotiations. Hanoi had always favoured that option as it excluded Saigon. Then, in May, Nixon offered Hanoi new peace terms. While still insistent that Thieu remain in power, he dropped Johnson's insistence that American troops would only withdraw six months after the NVA, and offered simultaneous withdrawal. He hinted that America would begin withdrawing soon anyway, as the ARVN was ready to take over. Hanoi was unimpressed. Why should they agree to withdraw if the Americans were going anyway? The North Vietnamese delegation said they were willing to sit in Paris 'until the chairs rot'. Nixon told Kissinger to warn the North Vietnamese in Paris that as America was withdrawing troops and was willing to accept the results of South Vietnamese elections, they must do likewise or Nixon would have to do something dramatic. Kissinger set them a 1 November deadline.

Hanoi answered that they had no troops in South Vietnam(!) and that Thieu must give way to a coalition government.

As he was making little progress with Hanoi, Nixon turned to Moscow. In October Nixon put pressure on the Soviets, promising detente for their help in ending the Vietnam war. He warned them not to reject this offer of more trade, arms control and decreased tension. 'The humiliation of a defeat is absolutely unacceptable to my country.' In 1969, diplomatically as well as militarily, Nixon was struggling. He had tried changes, concessions and threats, but seemed no nearer to peace. 1970 was no better.

Nixon's goals were clear. He wanted to be out of Vietnam before the presidential election of November 1972, leaving pro-American governments in South Vietnam, Cambodia and Laos. He also wanted Hanoi to release American prisoners of war (POWs). How was he to get this? His only means of persuasion were 'Mad Bomber' performances and linkage (linking American concessions to the USSR and China to their assistance in ending the Vietnam war). In spring 1971 it seemed as if linkage might be working. Nixon's planned rapprochement with both the USSR and China was becoming a reality. There were arms agreements with the Soviets and a Nixon visit to China in the pipeline. This affected Vietnam, as Nixon intended. The USSR and China were urging Hanoi not to insist on Thieu's removal as a prerequisite for peace. In May Nixon offered to get out by a set date without demanding mutual withdrawal. In return Hanoi should stop sending additional troops or materials to South Vietnam, observe a cease-fire, and guarantee the territorial integrity of Laos and Cambodia (just when the Communists were about to win in both). Thieu would have to stay in power and the American POWs would be returned. Hanoi was unimpressed, especially as there was no mention of stopping the bombing. At the end of 1971, Nixon's diplomatic offensives appeared to be as unproductive as his military ones. After three years, he seemed no nearer to obtaining peace with honour. Hanoi just would not give in.

c) The Home Front Problem

While Nixon put military and diplomatic pressure on the enemy, he used several tactics to keep the home front quiet. He made a series of American troop withdrawals from Vietnam. He timed the announcements to defuse public opposition, as in September 1969. Anti-war activists and congressmen were preparing to protest, so Nixon announced the withdrawal of 60,000 troops. Kissinger opposed the troop withdrawals, saying it would decrease American bargaining power with Hanoi and would be like giving salted peanuts to the American public - they would just want more and more. Nixon felt public opinion gave him little choice. He judged (rightly if cynically) that the heart of the anti-war movement was male college students threatened with the draft. He therefore adjusted it so that those over 20 were no longer threatened. This temporarily decreased protests and Nixon got a 71 per cent approval rating. He tried to keep his actions a secret in order to forestall the anti-war protesters, as with the 1969 bombing of Cambodia. When a British correspondent in Cambodia publicised it, Nixon, convinced it was an internal leak, ordered large-scale wiretapping.

Nixon also used speeches to keep the home front quiet and on 3 November 1969 delivered one of his best. He asked for time to end the war:

> And so tonight, to you, the great silent majority of my fellow Americans - I ask for your support. Let us be united for peace. Let us be united against defeat. Because let us understand: North Vietnam cannot defeat or humiliate the United States. Only Americans can do that.

The speech won universal acclaim, but although Nixon exulted, 'We've got those liberal bastards on the run now, and we're going to keep them on the run', protests soon began again. Nixon's speeches were not always truthful. In April 1970 he explained why he had sent American and ARVN troops into Cambodia. He said America had respected Cambodian neutrality for five years ('a whopper' says Ambrose). However, the Vietnamese Communists had vital bases there. Doing nothing would hurt America's troop withdrawal. The Communists might think they could escalate without American retaliation. 'This is not an invasion of Cambodia', just a clean-up operation. 'If, when the chips are down, the world's most powerful nation, the United States of America, acts like a pitiful, helpless giant, the forces of totalitarianism and anarchy will threaten free nations and free institutions throughout the world.' America's first defeat in its 190-year existence would be a national disgrace. This emotive language was effective. The speech proved quite popular, but again the success was short-lived.

Speeches, troop withdrawals, adjustments to the draft and (attempted) secrecy were insufficient to halt the protests. Nixon rightly claimed that the protesters were a minority, but their numbers were growing. In October 1969 the campuses were in uproar and the largest anti-war protest in American history took place. In this 'Moratorium' protesters took to the streets in every major city. Millions participated, many middle class and middle-aged. The more radical waved VC flags, chanted defeatist slogans and burned American flags. Although such behaviour proved unpopular, it made Nixon drop the 1 November ultimatum to Hanoi. He backed down to keep the public happy, despite saying that,

> to allow government policy to be made in the streets would destroy the democratic process. It would give the decision, not to the majority, and not to those with the strongest arguments, but to those with the

loudest voices. It would reduce statecraft to slogans. It would invite
5 anarchy.

Between 14 and 16 November, a quarter of a million peaceful
protesters took over Washington. Thousands of marchers carrying
candles filed past the White House, each saying the name of an
American soldier. Nixon wondered whether he could have thousands
of helicopters fly low over them to blow out their candles and drown
their voices. Simultaneously, news of the My Lai massacre (see page
89) surfaced. Although Nixon reminded everyone that the VC often
behaved similarly, many thought that if the price of war was making
murderers out of American youths, it was too high.

The Cambodian offensive caused trouble on campuses across
America. On 5 May 1970 four students at Kent State University, Ohio,
were shot dead by the National Guard. Some had been participating
in an anti-war rally, some just changing classes. Student protests escalated. All Californian colleges were closed down by the state governor.
As students rioted, Nixon backed down and declared he would get
American troops out of Cambodia by June. Again, government policy
was made in the streets. The military were furious. In New York City,
100,000 pro-Nixon people demonstrated and construction workers
(traditionally Democrats) beat up students from the East's leading
colleges in support of the Republican president's policies. Polls
showed how the Cambodian intervention had divided Americans: 50
per cent approved Nixon's Cambodian offensive, 39 per cent disapproved. As the Cambodian offensive appeared to be a dramatic escalation of the war authorised solely by the president, it aggravated relations between the president and Congress. Under pressure of the
Cold War, America had been developing what many historians call the
'imperial presidency', wherein the president had been acquiring near
absolute control over foreign policy. A congressional backlash was
inevitable, especially when presidential foreign policy was unpopular.
Throughout 1970 and 1971 the Senate enthusiastically supported
bills to stop Nixon waging war in Cambodia, Laos and Vietnam.
Congress rightly said the constitution gave them alone the power to
declare war and to raise and financially support the armed forces,
although Nixon also had a good point when he said that he had
inherited a war and the constitution gave him powers as commander-
in-chief. Nixon's time was running out. 'Virtually everybody wants
out,' said one hawk. Nixon could not get re-elected unless he got
America out, so why was he so slow? He could save neither Thieu, nor
honour, nor peace if he just got out. He desperately wanted a face-
saving formula that would get America out and leave Thieu in power
at least for a decent interval. Nixon told Republican senators, 'I will
not be the first President of the United States to lose a war.'
Vietnamisation and getting Russia and China to abandon Vietnam
were his great hopes, but it all took time and that was what Nixon

lacked. In 1971 Nixon's approval rating dropped to 31 per cent. Congress questioned Nixon about 'his' undemocratic ally. Johnson's constitution for Saigon had decreed a presidential election for October 1971. Thieu held it, but only allowed one candidate - himself! Some senators tried to halt all aid to South Vietnam unless there was a democratic election. Nixon could only say that democracy took time to develop.

One of Nixon's greatest problems was his own frustration when he failed to get domestic support. He became increasingly emotional, suspicious and vengeful. During the Cambodian offensive he told a Pentagon employee that the boys in Vietnam were the greatest, unlike the 'bums … blowing up the campuses'. Such language exacerbated American divisions. When his May 1970 attacks on North Vietnamese anti-aircraft facilities became public, he thought Secretary of Defence Laird and Secretary of State Rogers were the source of the 'leak' and therefore had them wiretapped. Not surprisingly, Hanoi itself had announced it! The pressure was clearly affecting Nixon's judgement. In 1971 the Pentagon Papers were published. This scrappy narrative of American involvement in Vietnam had been commissioned under McNamara. It showed the Democratic presidents in a poor light. Nixon was not bothered but Kissinger was. Kissinger had employed the man who leaked the documents. He told Nixon

> The fact that some idiot can publish all of the diplomatic secrets of this country … is damaging to your image … and it could destroy our ability to conduct foreign policy. It shows you're a weakling, Mr President.

That did it. Nixon was now even more determined to stop leaks. 'Anyone who opposes us, we'll destroy,' said a White House aide. 'As a matter of fact, anyone who doesn't support us, we'll destroy.' As it turned out, the search for leaks would help destroy both Nixon and South Vietnam.

After three years, then, a frustrated Nixon seemed no closer to bringing peace to America or Vietnam. Public opposition was hampering the military offensives he hoped would get Hanoi to make concessions at the peace talks. As yet, his diplomatic offensives were not paying off. The USSR and China could not or would not persuade Hanoi to give in. Aware of American national honour and credibility, and fearful of alienating the right-wing, Nixon insisted that Thieu remain in power. Hanoi would not agree to that.

4 1972 - Getting Re-elected

1972 was the presidential election year. Nixon needed some great breakthrough to ensure he won. He continued to use his traditional combination of military aggression and negotiation to try to end the war. In early 1972 it looked impossible.

a) Problems in Early 1972

In January 1972, Nixon's combination of military and diplomatic pressure still seemed unsuccessful. His bombing offensive on the North antagonised many Americans. Many US pilots were shot down during the air offensive, increasing the number of POWs held by Hanoi. Many congressmen were willing to abandon South Vietnam in exchange for the POWs, but Nixon used their existence and safety to help convince others of the need to continue the war.

The USSR and China were pressing Hanoi to settle, to let Nixon out with honour and to let Thieu remain for a while. However, Hanoi did not want to face a superbly equipped ARVN perpetually supplied by America, so the NVA began a great March offensive against South Vietnam, using tanks and artillery as never before. The ARVN crumbled. Nixon's policy of Vietnamisation was discredited in the presidential election year. He was furious with North Vietnam. He believed they had used negotiations as a smokescreen for this offensive. He was also angry with the USSR for providing the tanks and artillery. Kissinger tried to encourage Nixon. He argued that even if the NVA won while American troops pulled out, at least Nixon could claim credit for ending the war. Nixon said that possibility was 'too bleak even to contemplate'. Defeat was 'simply not an option'. He thought his political survival was impossible if he failed in Vietnam. He thought the credibility of American foreign policy would end with failure in Vietnam, and felt Kissinger underestimated the dangers therein. Nixon therefore ordered bombing of selected North Vietnamese targets: these 'bastards have never been bombed like they are going to be bombed this time'. B-52 bombers were used in North Vietnam for the first time since 1968 and inflicted heavy casualties, but nevertheless the NVA still advanced. Nixon wanted to escalate the bombing. Laird feared the Soviet anti-aircraft defences, congressional reaction, and the possible loss of a planned summit with the Soviets but Nixon went ahead. He bombed oil depots around Hanoi and Haiphong: 'we really left them our calling card this weekend'. Nixon successfully divided Hanoi and Moscow by threatening the latter with cancellation of the summit. On 16 April American bombers hit four Soviet merchant ships at anchor in Haiphong, but the Soviets were so keen to have the summit, that their protests were low-key. Linkage was working. 'The summit is not worth a damn if the price for it is losing in Vietnam,' said Nixon. 'My instinct tells me that the country can take losing a summit, but it can't take losing the war.' However, Kissinger gave detente priority and on his own initiative hinted to the Soviets that America might consider a coalition government without a North Vietnamese withdrawal. Kissinger knew concessions were essential if the war were to be brought to an end and was now more inclined to compromise than Nixon. He was being ostracised by old Harvard colleagues, and was terrified he might suffer the fate of one of Johnson's academic advisers, who on returning to academia was banished to the University of Texas!

Nixon meanwhile decided to mine North Vietnam's ports. He said,

If the United States betrays the millions of people who have relied on us in Vietnam ... it would amount to renunciation of our morality, an abdication of our leadership among nations, and an invitation for the mighty to prey upon the meek all around the world.

He said if America was strong, the world would remain half instead of wholly Communist. The Democrats were critical: one spoke of flirting with World War Three to keep General Thieu in power and save Nixon's face for a little longer. However, it was Nixon who understood the Soviets best. Moscow was tired of financing Hanoi's war and would not sacrifice the summit over the mining of their ally's ports. Nixon had made his position clear to Hanoi and Moscow. He would not destroy Hanoi (there was no talk of using atomic weapons) but he could hurt it. Nor would he abandon Thieu, even at the cost of losing the summit. However, he was hinting to Moscow a new willingness to accept a coalition containing Communists - a great concession. Nixon continued the bombing throughout the summit, illustrating one of the ways in which he intended to get America out of Vietnam 'with honour' - by disguising concessions with simultaneous shows of force. Nixon's approval rating shot up. As the Soviets and Chinese pressed Hanoi to settle, Hanoi rightly accused them of putting their own interests above those of world revolution. However, America was offering Hanoi yet another vital concession: the NVA would be allowed to stay in South Vietnam, which would be crucial to their future victory.

Hanoi was finally being driven toward a settlement by a combination of American concessions, pressure from their allies, the failure of their offensive to take big cities, Operation Phoenix (see page 89), the destructiveness of the B-52s, and the probable re-election of the unpredictable Mad Bomber. After three years, Nixon's combination of military and diplomatic pressure and concessions appeared to be working. It was just as well. He did not have much longer.

b) Autumn 1972: Running Out of Time and Money

By the second half of 1972 Nixon was running out of time and money. Troop withdrawals meant that Congress could no longer be shamed into granting funds to help 'our boys in the field'. Nixon begged them not to damage his negotiating capabilities, and pointed out that just walking away from Vietnam would lead to a blood bath for former Thieu supporters. Allowing that to happen would be the height of immorality. Polls showed most Americans agreed with Nixon's bottom line. 55 per cent supported continued heavy bombing of North Vietnam, 64 per cent the mining of Haiphong and 74 per cent thought it important that South Vietnam should not fall to the

Communists. Nixon told Kissinger to tell the Vietnamese negotiator
Le Duc Tho he had had enough:

> Settle or else! ... No nonsense. No niceness. No accommodations ...
> tell those sons of bitches that the President is a madman and you don't
> know how to deal with him. Once re-elected I'll be a mad bomber.

Despite this tough talk, both sides were compromising. It seemed
Hanoi would let Thieu remain in power while America would let the
NVA stay in South Vietnam and not insist upon a cease-fire in
Cambodia and Laos. However, Hanoi insisted upon a voice in the
Saigon government and there seemed no chance of Thieu accepting
that, despite Nixon's promise that America would never desert him.
Kissinger rejected the idea of a coalition government but offered a
Committee of National Reconciliation (to be one third South
Vietnamese, one third Communist and one third neutral) to oversee
the constitution and elections. Kissinger thereby agreed that the
Communists were a legitimate political force in South Vietnam, which
Thieu had always denied. Kissinger ignored the tearful Thieu, while
Nixon reminded the latter of what had happened to Diem and
muttered 'the tail can't wag the dog'.

In October Kissinger thought he had an agreement. America would
withdraw all its armed forces but continue to supply the ARVN; there
would be a National Council of Reconciliation with Communist representation; the American POWs would be released; Thieu would
remain in power; the NVA would remain in South Vietnam; America
would help the economic reconstruction of North Vietnam as a
humanitarian gesture. Nixon said it was 'a complete capitulation by
the enemy' but then got cold feet and rejected the terms. Why? He
was worried about accusations that peace at this time was an electoral
ploy. He feared it would appear he had given in to people like
Hollywood's Jane Fonda, who had journeyed to Hanoi to express
shame at her country's deeds. Some advisers feared if peace came
before the election, people might vote Democrat as the Democrats
were supposedly better at peacetime governing, while Republicans
were good for foreign crises. The American right-wing opposed the
National Council. Most important of all and not surprisingly, Thieu
rejected the settlement and Nixon shared his doubts. Nixon was not
sure that this constituted peace with honour. Thieu wanted the NVA
out of South Vietnam and loathed the National Council. Nixon nevertheless felt his ally had to make some concessions and threatened him
with the withdrawal of American support. 'We're going to have to put
him through the wringer ... We simply have to cut the umbilical cord
and have this baby walk by itself.' The exasperated Kissinger called
Thieu 'a complete son of a bitch'.

Kissinger was as keen as Nixon for the latter to get re-elected. It
meant four more years for both of them. On the eve of the American
presidential election, Kissinger assured the press that 'Peace is at

hand.' A few 'minor details' needed tidying up. That statement infuriated Nixon who felt it would make Hanoi and Thieu more intransi-
gent. Nixon also resented Kissinger getting the glory from the
announcement. Some Democrats were cynical. Why was peace
suddenly at hand on the eve of the election? Nixon had had four years
to do this. Kissinger pointed out that Hanoi's recent concessions
allowing Thieu to remain in power were the difference. He omitted to
mention the American had also made concessions. Meanwhile Nixon
intensified the bombing to keep the pressure on Hanoi.

In November 1972 Nixon was re-elected but the new Democratic
Congress was not going to carry on funding the war. Nixon had done
all he could to help Thieu but his money would soon run out, so the
only way forward was to force Thieu to accept the unacceptable.
Nixon had just weeks to finish the war. He gave Thieu his 'absolute
assurance' that if Hanoi broke the peace, he would take 'swift and
severe retaliatory action'. Thieu knew that any agreement was
inevitably going to be a temporary cease-fire, so long as the NVA
remained in South Vietnam and that the American political system
could invalidate Nixon's promise of future aid against North
Vietnamese aggression. Some of Kissinger's staff were so exasperated
by Thieu's stubbornness that they suggested assassinating him! Le
Duc Tho was still willing to accept the October agreement which
Nixon and Kissinger had initially considered satisfactory. However,
having once rejected that agreement, America could hardly accept it
now without looking rather foolish.

On 18 December Nixon bombed and mined Haiphong again,
confiding to his diary that Hanoi thought 'they have us where the hair
is short and are going to continue to squeeze us', so he had to do
something. There was no public explanation for this Christmas 1972
bombing which caused worldwide uproar. Had not Kissinger promised
peace? Although American planes tried to avoid civilian casualties in
Hanoi, 1,000 died. The North Vietnamese shot down 15 B-52s with 93
American airmen, a rate of losses the US air force could not sustain for
long. Kissinger was cracking: he leaked to the press that he opposed
the bombing, which was untrue. One adviser thought that 'we look
incompetent - bombing for no good reason and because we do not
know what else to do'. What was the point? Was Nixon trying to reas-
sure Thieu of American strength and support? To weaken Hanoi so it
could not speedily threaten South Vietnam after peace was concluded?
Trying to disguise American retreats and compromises in the negotiations? Or had he lost control? It was perhaps a mixture of all those
reasons. Given the importance Nixon attached to military pressure,
the first two suggestions were probably the most important.
Nevertheless several congressmen and influential newspapers questioned Nixon's sanity and accused him of waging 'war by tantrum'.

It is difficult to see what the Christmas bombing had achieved. The
accord that was finally reached in Paris in January 1973 was basically

the same as that of October 1972 with a few cosmetic changes for both sides. Knowing his funding would soon be cut off, Nixon had to tell Thieu he was going to sign with or without him. On 22 January Thieu agreed, although he regarded it as virtual surrender.

The 27 January 1973 Paris peace accords declared a cease-fire throughout Vietnam (but not Cambodia nor Laos). POWs would be exchanged, after which America would remove the last of its troops. The NVA was not required to leave the South but had to promise not to 'take advantage' of the cease-fire, nor increase their numbers. Thieu remained in power, but the Committee of National Reconciliation contained Communist representation, and would sponsor free elections. Nixon secretly promised billions of dollars worth of reconstruction aid to Hanoi.

5 Success or Failure?

Kissinger and Le Duc Tho were awarded the highly prestigious Nobel peace prize for ending the Vietnam war. Did Kissinger deserve it more than Nixon? It was surely a true team effort. Did either of them really deserve a peace prize? Was Nixon a diplomatic genius or a mad bomber? His sanity was publicly questioned during the 1972 Christmas bombing. A Kissinger aide who quietly resigned over the 1970 Cambodian invasion, subsequently regretted his loyal decision not to call a press conference:

> I knew the administration was squalid. But there still was this enormous illusion about Henry. I clung to the delusion that the man was still rational ... it was my theory of the limits of the ruthlessness of Henry Kissinger; in truth, there were no limits.

However, looking at all that Nixon and Kissinger did, it is not difficult to find reasons for their actions. They were motivated by the desire to do what they thought was best for America, which for the most part was what they thought was best for themselves also. Although one might not agree with their interpretation, and although one might be particularly upset by what it meant for the victims of their slow withdrawal and saturation bombing, one cannot help but conclude that all was accomplished with rational calculation of what was politically acceptable and best for America and the western world.

Why did Nixon take so long to get out of Vietnam? During 1968, he had decided that America had to get out but it took him four years to do it, during which time 300,000 Vietnamese and 20,000 Americans died. Most of the names on the left-hand side of the Vietnam war memorial wall in Washington died during Nixon's presidency, in a war he had decided from the first he could not win. Having decided upon retreat, would it not have been less painful if Nixon had done it speedily? The slow retreat ensured a dramatic drop in the morale of American forces in Vietnam. It antagonised American anti-war

activists. It created the division, discontent and the presidential para-
noia that helped bring about Watergate (see page 130). However,
Nixon had his own good reasons for simply not getting out. In 1969
Hanoi was unwilling to accept that Thieu would remain in power.
Washington was wedded to Thieu because it recalled how South
Vietnam had neared disintegration after Diem. This did not seem the
time to change governments. Nixon felt American honour required
that Thieu's South Vietnam be left with a good chance of survival.
Why else had America fought at such great cost in men and money?
Nixon wrote to Rogers: 'We simply cannot tell the mothers of our
casualties and the soldiers who have spent part of their lives in
Vietnam that it was all to no purpose.' American national pride was at
stake. The country could not afford to be seen to be defeated. In a
November 1969 speech Nixon said he could have ended the war
immediately and blamed it all on Johnson. 'This was the only way to
avoid allowing Johnson's war to become Nixon's war.' But he had
bigger things to think about. He was convinced that a first American
defeat would lead to a collapse of confidence in American leadership
and to Communist expansion throughout the world. He was adamant
that South Vietnam's right to decide its future was not negotiable. He
wanted peace, but not at any price. He asked 'the great silent
majority' to support him because 'North Vietnam cannot defeat or
humiliate the United States. Only Americans can do that.' After that
'great silent majority' speech, Nixon's support soared to 68 per cent.
Although the slow withdrawal was painful, there were clearly many
who understood what Nixon was trying to do and sympathised with
him. Like so many Americans, Nixon genuinely believed that the
USSR and China presented a threat to America and its allies. Given
the lack of political freedom within those two countries and Eastern
Europe, those American fears were comprehensible and vital to
understanding why America got into Vietnam and insisted on getting
out 'with honour'. Kissinger said,

1   However we got into Vietnam, whatever the judgement of our actions,
    ending the war honourably ... [was] essential for the peace of the
    world. Any other solution may [have] unloose[d] forces that would
    [have] complicate[d] the prospects of international order ... For nearly
5   a generation the security and progress of free peoples had depended on
    confidence in America. We could not simply walk away from an enter-
    prise involving two administrations, five allied countries, and 31,000
    dead as if we were switching a TV channel ... As the leader of demo-
    cratic alliances we had to remember that scores of countries and
10 millions of people relied for their security on our willingness to stand
    by allies ... We could not revitalise the Atlantic alliance ... We would
    not be able to move the Soviet Union toward the imperative of mutual
    restraint ... We might not achieve our opening to China [if America lost
    credibility over Vietnam].

Although Kissinger and Nixon believed in detente, they thought it was dangerous if the Soviets and Chinese thought America was weak and they were probably right.

Does Nixon deserve any credit for the withdrawal? At the very least Nixon's critics have to admit that he got the American troops out of Vietnam. He did not always get much thanks for it (droves criticised his slowness) and he perhaps did not have much choice, but it was very significant indeed. It was difficult for any president to preside over the retreat of American power. Perhaps retreat from America's uncompromising and impossibly expensive Cold War militancy was one of Nixon's greatest achievements.

Had Nixon gained peace with honour? He had got the American ground forces out without abandoning Saigon. He had forced Hanoi to agree that Thieu could remain in power with the world's fourth largest air force and an improved ARVN. On the other hand, Nixon had aimed to get the NVA to withdraw and to nullify the VC in South Vietnam, but he had failed to do so. By late 1972 his freedom was limited: he knew Congress would cut off his money early in 1973, so that he had to make peace on whatever terms he could get and thanks to his 'mad bomber' and linkage tactics the terms were quite probably better than he could have got in 1969.

What did the peace cost Nixon? Perhaps the presidency itself. The difficulties of gaining 'peace with honour' in the face of domestic opposition and Vietnamese intransigence accentuated his tendency toward a siege mentality. During 1972 Nixon's Campaign to Re-elect the President (CREEP) indulged in dirty tricks and got caught breaking into the Democrats' offices in the Watergate building. The scandal simmered relatively quietly in late 1972 but during Nixon's second term, it exploded and brought the president down. Many Americans believed that had Nixon not felt besieged and battered by the Vietnam war, had he not believed that Vietnam might cost him re-election, Watergate would not have happened.

Had Nixon really won peace for Indochina in January 1973? No. The fighting continued in South Vietnam. Thieu's interpretation of the cease-fire was clear: 'If Communists come into your village, you should immediately shoot them in the head.' Nixon bombed Communist sanctuaries in Cambodia until 15 August 1973 when his money was cut off. Within months, Cambodia had become Communist, and so had South Vietnam. North Vietnam overran South Vietnam in 1975. There was no help from America. Nixon had resigned because of Watergate in 1974. Had he still been president, would Nixon have saved Saigon? Or had he (like Kissinger) just wanted a decent interval to elapse before the inevitable Saigon collapse? In 1977 Nixon told David Frost that he did not think he could have saved South Vietnam because Congress was opposed to any more American actions there. Nixon's expensively gained 'peace with honour' was thus untenable. The foreign policy genius had failed to engineer the domestic consensus necessary to save the incompetent Thieu.

Summary Diagram
'Richard Nixon, Diplomatic Genius or Mad Bomber?'

Why Nixon Ended the War				
Unwinnable	Cold War Changed	American Anti-War Movement	Vote-Winner	Congressional opposition

How Nixon Ended the War		
Kissinger's diplomacy	Linkage - enticed USSR and China to put pressure on Hanoi	Military pressure - bombed North Vietnam and trail in Cambodia and Laos. Mad Bomber!

Why peace took so long
Washington and Hanoi unwilling to make concessions - both sought Peace with Honour

Making notes on 'Richard Nixon, Diplomatic Genius or Mad Bomber'

Nixon's retreat from Vietnam lends itself to structured essay questions, so make detailed notes on the topics and debates upon which you are most likely to be questioned, i) why Nixon decided to end the war, ii) his strategy for doing so, iii) why he took so long to end the war, iv) how he ended it and v) whether the peace was 'peace with honour'. You could also list points for and against Nixon's 'secrecy, duplicity, and ... ruthless attention to immediate political advantage regardless of larger moral issues'. Similar notes could be made to assist revision of the other presidents. The sections on 'immediate political advantage' will give you many ideas about the difficulties of conducting foreign policy in a democracy.

Answering essay questions on 'Richard Nixon, Diplomatic Genius or Mad Bomber'

Some questions might require knowledge of Johnson as well as Nixon, for example,

1. How and/or why did America retreat from the Vietnam war?
2. What problems faced America in trying to obtain a peace settlement in Vietnam?

These are 'pure' Nixon questions in ascending order of difficulty:

3. **a)** Why did Nixon decide to end the war? (6 marks)
    b) Why did it take Nixon four years to end it? (10 marks)
    c) Did he obtain a good peace settlement? (9 marks)
4. **a)** To what extent was Nixon's strategy for getting America out of the Vietnam war successful? (15 marks)
    b) How important was Kissinger to Nixon's Vietnam policy? (10 marks)
5. To what extent was Nixon's Vietnam policy characterised by 'ruthless attention to immediate political advantage'?
6. In retirement Nixon said his 'biggest mistake' had been not bombing North Vietnam from the first. Would you agree?

Questions 3c, 4a and 5 ask you to evaluate claims. 'To what extent' and 'how far' are the examiner's helpful (yes!) ways of suggesting that there are several possible answers to a controversial question, and you are being invited to demonstrate that you have mastered all of them. When asked to evaluate the peace settlement of January 1973 from the American point of view for example, you would look at the advantages for America (all troops and POWs out, 'face' saved by the retention of Thieu, money saved, domestic divisions decreased) but also the disadvantages (Nixon's promise to help Thieu in future, allowing Communist forces to remain in South Vietnam and to have political recognition). You would then conclude whether or not the advantages outweighed the disadvantages. There is not necessarily a 'right' answer: you just have to look at both sides and then give reasonable arguments to sustain your conclusion.

Source-based questions on 'Richard Nixon, Diplomatic Genius or Mad Bomber?'

1. Nixon's motivation in Vietnam

Look at the extracts from Nixon on page 113 and page 125, and Kissinger on page 129. Answer the following questions.

a) Name any three of the 'five allied countries' mentioned by Kissinger. (3 marks)
b) To what extent do these sources differ in their views of China and the USSR? (5 marks)

c) Would you describe the tone of these three extracts as idealistic? Explain your answer. (5 marks)

d) What are the strengths and weaknesses of the second source as evidence about why Nixon mined North Vietnam's ports? (4 marks)

e) Using the sources and your background knowledge, explain why Nixon fought so hard for 'peace with honour'. (8 marks)

9 Conclusions

1 The Debates

The previous chapters have identified the issues which historians have debated on the topic of America and Vietnam. Why did America get involved in Vietnam? Which president was mainly responsible for the involvement? Should presidents take all the responsibility? Why could America not achieve her great aim of an independent South Vietnam? Why was America so slow to get out of Vietnam? What, if anything, had America achieved? Some suggestions are given below. If and when you find yourself disagreeing with anything that is said, you should be able to give reasons to substantiate your view. You might spot some omissions of points that you consider important.

Why did America get involved in Vietnam? Successive presidents viewed the world through a Cold War perspective which made a Communist victory in Vietnam seem very significant. In reality though, Ho Chi Minh and his followers were nationalists first and Communists second. They were not the puppets of Moscow or Beijing. However, successive administrations believed a Communist Vietnam would affect the world balance of power in favour of Communism and cause other Southeast Asian 'dominoes' to fall. Was American motivation therefore primarily ideological? Or were naked power and greed equally important?

Which president was responsible for the involvement? Is it reasonable to claim that they all bore responsibility? Truman aided the French. Eisenhower was vital in the establishment of South Vietnam and he and Kennedy propped up Diem. Kennedy's complicity in the fall of Diem increased America's obligation to his Saigon successors in the minds of Johnson and others. Once American money and lives had been expended, it seemed a betrayal of all who had gone before to withdraw. It was always hoped that 'just a little more' effort would do the trick. It was very difficult for any president to get out, as his predecessors had bequeathed him a commitment which seemed to have developed into a moral obligation. So, should each of the presidents involved shoulder the same amount of blame?

Should the presidents bear all the blame? All presidents had advisers such as Acheson, Dulles, McNamara and Kissinger who encouraged the commitment to South Vietnam. Congress, the public and the press were supportive for much of the time, which is particularly apparent during Johnson's escalation. However, is there any justification in the argument that the person at the top should always 'carry the can'?

Why could America not achieve her great aim of permanently establishing an independent South Vietnam? Hanoi got invaluable support from Moscow and Beijing. The Communists fought with incredible tenacity. As Kissinger said, 'The conventional army loses if it does not win; the guerrilla wins if he does not lose.' Giap used a judicious mixture of guerrilla and conventional warfare. The guerrillas were never going to give up. They were sufficiently attractive and/or threatening to the Vietnamese peasants to gain the support necessary for survival. The Americans fought a limited war in which their tactics served to aid Communist popularity. Their South Vietnamese allies were usually corrupt, inefficient and unpopular. The American home front collapsed, and the morale of the American army plummeted from 1968 onwards. American politicians decided the war had to stop. So, did America lose the war at home rather than in Vietnam?

Why was America so slow to get out of Vietnam? American power, prestige, credibility and security seemed likely to suffer if the country was seen to be defeated. Retreat would also alienate many American electors, whose (supposed) wishes help to explain the involvement, escalation and withdrawal. Was the American retreat (and the American involvement) dominated by the presidential desire to placate the electorate?

There are other questions that need to be considered. One of the most important of these is, 'What were the effects of the Vietnam War?'

2 The Effects of the War

a) Death and Destruction

Three million Americans served in Vietnam: about 46,000 were killed in action, 10,000 died through accidents, and around 300,000 were wounded. Over 5,000 Allied troops died: 4,407 South Koreans, 469 Australians and New Zealanders, and 350 Thais. 137,000 ARVN were killed and 300,000 were wounded. Around 400,000 South Vietnamese civilians died and three quarters of a million were wounded. Giap admitted to 600,000 North Vietnamese losses, but America claimed 800,000 died in the NVA and one million VC. Around two and a half million Vietnamese died and one and a half million were wounded out of the total population of about 32 million.

For the survivors and their families, many mental and physical wounds remain. 'Now it's all gone down the drain and it hurts. What did he die for?' asked the parent of an American soldier. Divisions and resentment are very much alive in America. A survey of veterans in 1988 suggested that half a million of the three million Americans who had served in Vietnam suffered from 'post-traumatic stress disorder'. Symptoms could appear 10 to 15 years later, including panic, rage, anxiety, depression and emotional paralysis. Divorce, suicide, drug addiction and particularly alcoholism are higher than average among veterans. One veterans' attempt to heal themselves and the nation was the construction of the Vietnam war memorial in Washington. There were bitter arguments about its existence and design. A sombre, long, black slash of marble, like a deep wound in the ground, it contains the names of more than 56,000 Americans who died in Vietnam.

In Vietnam, there are victims of American napalm who were melted into a kind of gelatine. Some hideously disfigured survivors slunk off to live in caves or remote areas. Vietnam cannot afford cosmetic surgery for them. American ecological warfare had a tremendous impact. The incidence of cancer and toxin-related diseases is unusually high in Vietnam because of American spraying of herbicides such as Agent Orange, which contained dioxin. Much forest and agricultural land was ruined. By the end of the war, extensive areas had been taken over by tough weeds which the locals call 'American grass'. Since the end of the war, thousands of Vietnamese have been killed by unexploded bombs, shells and land-mines while clearing land or ploughing their fields. Some make a precarious living by collecting this scrap metal although remaining White Phosphorous artillery shells still terrify them. If they explode, the chemical burns through to the bone and can only be removed with something like a metal razor blade.

b) Vietnam's Economic and Social Problems

The tremendous unity of purpose and sense of mission which characterised the North in the war seemed to disappear after it. Giap admitted that the Communist Party leadership was better at waging war than running a country. For more than 20 years after the Americans withdrew Vietnam remained one of the world's poorest nations thanks to the legacy of war damage coupled with unsuccessful Communist economic policies. After 1975 the victorious government in Hanoi was divided, some favouring traditional Marxist-Leninist revolutionary dogmas, others inclined more to flexibility. The problems facing a united government would have been bad enough: a shattered economy, social and political divisions, exhausted people, ruined urban and rural areas.

After 1975 the victorious Communists concentrated upon heavy industry (like the early USSR) but lacked the necessary capital and skills. Communist economic policies removed the stimulation of money-making incentives. Even Saigon's hairdressers were collectivised. The rapidly growing population (which had tripled since 1930) could not be fed. Southern peasants were disillusioned by the collectivisation of farm land and in the fertile Mekong Delta they preferred to sell their produce on the black market rather than hand it over to government agencies. Some slaughtered their water buffalo rather than give them to the government, or let land lie fallow rather than cultivate crops for the government. Even fish became scarce as thousands of 'boat people' fled the country in fishing boats.

Vietnamese society was badly dislocated by the war. Many anti-Communist Vietnamese fled the country. The massive exodus of 'boat people' was one of the biggest twentieth-century migrations. Over one million left between 1975 and 1990. Many died from exposure or drowning. Now over three-quarters of a million of them live in America, one million in other western countries, but hundreds of thousands spent years in squalid refugee camps in Thailand, Malaysia, the Philippines and Hong Kong. Unless they could prove they fled for political rather than economic reasons, they were often repatriated, especially by the British authorities in Hong Kong. Another quarter of a million ethnic Chinese fled the new Vietnam for China. Some did not get out in time or found it hard to leave. Around 50,000 'Amerasian' children remained as a visible reminder of the American presence. Some blond and blue eyed, some black, all were treated as outcasts and reduced to begging or prostitution. By 1990, 30,000 had gone to America.

Political divisions were hard to overcome. The new government persecuted those associated with the old regime. 300,000 South Vietnamese civil servants, army officers, doctors, lawyers and intellectuals were 're-educated' in concentration camps where malaria, dysentery, torture and executions were common. World pressure meant that by 1990 most of the survivors were released for emigration to the United States. This loss of skilled labour was a national tragedy. Some who had been pro-Communist during the war became bitter in peacetime. When Stanley Karnow returned to Communist Vietnam in 1990 he looked up many old friends. He was surprised to find that some influential individuals in Saigon had actually been Communist agents. They told him their motivation had been nationalism but that they had become disillusioned with the Communist regime after 1975. One old friend told him how wives of Communist leaders flew from Hanoi to Ho Chi Minh City (the victors' name for Saigon) aboard army planes to buy up heirlooms from once-rich families at bargain prices. Karnow said that abuse of rank reminded him of the wives of the Saigon generals during the war. 'Exactly,' said his friend, 'this is still very much a feudal society, whatever its ideological labels.'

c) Vietnam's Foreign Friends and Enemies

During the war Vietnamese relations with the USSR and China were good, but once the war was over, old Sino-Vietnamese hostilities erupted, culminating in war in 1979. Ironically, America, which had got involved in Vietnam partly or mostly to contain China, supported China against Vietnam. This left Vietnam totally dependent upon Soviet aid. 4,000 Russians were sent to rebuild the Vietnamese economy. The Vietnamese called them 'Americans without dollars' - poor and bossy invaders. A favourite Vietnamese joke told of Hanoi begging Moscow for economic aid, to which Moscow replied,

'Tighten your belts.' 'Send belts', was the Vietnamese answer. The collapse of the USSR meant the cessation of Soviet aid in 1991, making the Russians the people most hated by the Vietnamese today. Ironically again, Hanoi became desperate for improved relations with America, hoping to get trade and aid.

The resumption of normal relations between America and Vietnam were thwarted by residual bitterness in Washington, fuelled by the supposed MIAs (missing in action). Finding the dead bodies of American soldiers who were unaccounted for was difficult with the terrain and climate of Vietnam. Bodies decay rapidly in the tropics. American politicians, the media and families were generally reluctant to give up on these men. After the war, 62 per cent of Americans believed the MIAs were still being held prisoner by Hanoi. Politicians and the media were probably motivated by self-interest. It was a good story, and politicians were uneasy about the emotions they would arouse if they were to say 'forget it'. The Americans sent teams to search for American bodies buried in Vietnamese cemeteries. Hanoi was willing to allow this as they wanted better diplomatic relations and the Americans paid Vietnamese workers high wages to dig up corpses. However, ordinary Vietnamese were offended when their relations were dug up in the search. In America it was difficult to overcome the bitter memories of the unsuccessful war with those whom Kissinger called 'the most bloody-minded bastards' he had ever known. In 1991 America stopped the International Monetary Fund granting economic aid to Vietnam and a British newspaper said, 'One day Vietnam may overcome the consequences of having won its war against America. The Americans are putting off this day as long as possible.' In 1994 President Bill Clinton, although highly sensitive about his own 'draft-dodging' in the war (it was a big issue in his election campaign), nevertheless moved the process of reconciliation forward. In July 1995 he declared he would re-establish diplomatic relations. American businessmen were very interested in Vietnam but cultural misunderstandings remained. An American plan to open a chain entitled 'Uncle Ho's Hamburgers' was considered highly offensive.

d) Vietnam in the late 1990s

When looking back on the wars in Vietnam, it is not always easy to decide what they were about. There was a nationalist war of independence against the colonialist French and then, according to Hanoi, against the imperialist Americans. There was also a civil war between Vietnamese to decide what the future of Vietnam should be. Ho's Communism was in many ways a distillation of the conservative peasant community spirit, but opposing it were the ideas of freer and more individualistic spirits in the South, especially Saigon with its dynamic capitalist urban middle class. In 1975 the communal spirit seemed to have triumphed, partly because of its close association with old traditions, but mostly because of its association with nationalism. The removal of foreign threats meant a loss of dynamism for the Communist way, and 1990s Western tourists seeing the revival of a capitalist economy and the vulgarity of Ho Chi Minh City wondered whether the South had not won after all. In Ho Chi Minh City, local Communist chiefs ran brothels and the crime rate was as high as in the old Saigon days. Influenced by Soviet reforms in the late 1980s and Chinese reforms in the 1990s, Hanoi introduced greater economic flexibility in order to improve their disastrous situation. The market economy, private ownership and incentives made a dramatic comeback. The peasants responded to incentives and Vietnam became one of the Third World's largest rice exporters. Vietnam also became a trendy tourist venue. Western tourists were keen to see what remained of its unspoiled Third World backwardness as well as its beautiful scenery. Tourists reported the triumph of capitalistic practices, particularly in Ho Chi Minh City which, apart from the name, was not so very different from its American days. The locals wore American-style T-shirts and jeans, and the black market still flourished. Officials throughout Vietnam were frequently corrupt and enjoyed giving 'spot' fines to hapless Western tourists, perhaps being made to pay for the sins of their predecessors.

e) The Vietnam War and the Cold War

It is difficult to decide whether the Vietnam War, which grew out of the Cold War, had a marked impact on that latter conflict. The Soviets and Chinese improved relations with America even as Nixon bombed Hanoi but the improvement might not have happened had they not known that Nixon was getting the American troops out. Outside of Indochina, the dominoes did not fall to Communism during the Vietnam war nor after it, which might or might not have been due to the American effort. Many potential dominoes prospered. South Korea in particular did very well out of the war, selling vast quantities of goods to the Americans. America, however, will probably never be the same again. The Vietnam war certainly weakened America, although America still remains the world's greatest military power. However, America lost its unrivalled world economic leadership and Americans lost much of their unquestioning belief in their nation's cultural rectitude and supremacy. The confidence and optimism born of two triumphant world wars (and to a lesser extent Korea) was lost. Governments and people were more hesitant about future involvement in international relations. The first Reagan administration (1981-85) saw a massive arms build-up and much Cold War rhetoric, but in order to get re-elected Reagan had to take a more moderate line. Polls in the 1980s showed the American public carefully watching Central American events to stop 'another Vietnam'. When the Bush administration got involved in the 1991 Gulf war, Congress debated long and hard and only endorsed entry by a narrow margin. Speedy military success in the Gulf caused a jubilant President George Bush to claim that, 'By God, we've kicked the Vietnam syndrome once and for all.' The Gulf war demonstrated that the American military had recovered from the traumatic Vietnam years. However, as it became clearer that the problems in the Gulf had not been totally solved, it seemed likely that Bush's optimism was unjustified.

3 Is it Important to Study this Topic?

The great American car manufacturer Henry Ford said, 'History is bunk.' Sometimes people find it hard to understand why anyone should investigate or read about events which happened years ago. Should Americans investigate and understand Vietnam? Do men like my uncle and his family need to know why America fought and lost in order to make sense of what happened to them? Most Americans consider Vietnam was a mistake. Ought all potential voters in the American democracy to understand what happened in the hope that they can exercise their political rights to ensure it does not happen again? You might ask yourselves why you bother to study history, and why this particular part of it. American culture is highly influential throughout the world, and particularly in countries which share the same language. Do we need to understand America and to develop awareness of the workings of politics and international relations? Might it help us to understand our relationship with Ireland or Europe? If the answer to those questions is yes, problems still remain. We do not all look at the same historical experience with the same eyes. It is not that easy to learn from history. Johnson and his contemporaries thought that they had learned the right lesson from the appeasement of Hitler during the 1930s and that they could apply it to Vietnam. It seems that they were wrong. Is the final tragedy of the Vietnam war that it developed out of a combination of ideas, people and events so unusual and complex that we cannot make sufficient sense out of it to find an agreed lesson to learn from it? At the very least can we say that any democracy should take great care not to get involved in a foreign country without exhaustive domestic debate to ensure consensus, without considerable knowledge of that country and its history, and without detailed study of a war like America's in Vietnam?

Working on the Conclusion

You will not need many notes on this conclusion which for the most part simply tries to finish off the story, although you might want to make a brief list of the results of the war. The sub-section on 'debates' might help in revision of 'America and Vietnam'. When revising, you could use the summary questions posed as issues around which to build a final set of summarising notes of your own.

Summary Diagram
'Conclusions'

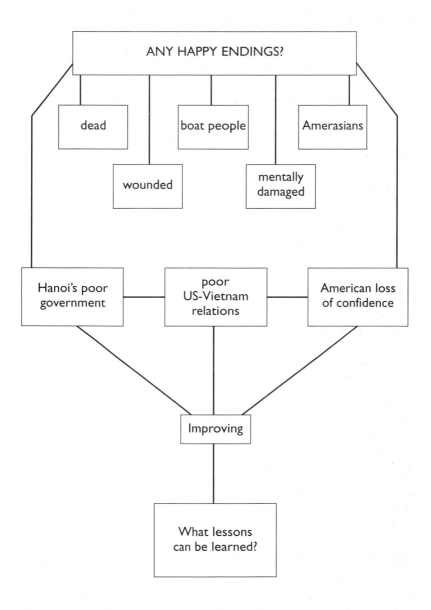

Chronological Table

1428	Chinese recognised Vietnamese independence.
1600s	French missionaries arrived in Vietnam.
1820	First American arrived in Vietnam to trade.
1887	French created Indochinese Union.
1919	Woodrow Wilson ignored Ho Chi Minh's petition for Vietnamese independence from France during the Paris Peace Conference.
1930	Ho founded Indochinese Communist Party.
1939-45	Japanese occupied French Indochina for most of the Second World War.
1944	Americans co-operated with Ho against Japanese.
1945	July - Truman agreed that Britain and China could take Japan's surrender in French Indochina.
	September - Ho declared Vietnamese independence.
	Truman made no objection when Britain allowed France to return to Indochina.
1950	January - Truman refused to recognise Ho's Democratic Republic of Vietnam but Communist China and the USSR did so.
	June - Communist North Korea attacked America's protégé South Korea.
	July - Truman granted $15 million aid to France for fighting Communism in Indochina.
1954	April - Eisenhower decided against American intervention to help France at Dien Bien Phu after Britain and Congress unenthusiastic.
	May - July - Geneva conference on Indochina temporarily divided Indochina. Accepted by all except US which felt Ho had been given too much.
	September - US organised SEATO (Southeast Asia Treaty Organisation) with Britain, France, Australia, New Zealand, Pakistan, Thailand and the Philippines. Would help any anti-Communist Vietnamese.
	October - US promised $100 million to Diem, leader of anti-Communist regime in southern Vietnam.
1955	July - Diem rejected Geneva agreements on nationwide elections. Americans supported him.
	October - Diem proclaimed Republic of Vietnam with himself as president. US promised to help him train his army (ARVN). Now effectively two Vietnamese states, North Vietnam and South Vietnam.
1957	Communist insurgency began in South Vietnam.
1959	North Vietnamese sent men and weapons into South Vietnam via Ho Chi Minh Trail.
1960	Hanoi formed National Liberation Front against South Vietnam - Diem called them VC (Vietcong or

Vietnamese Communists).

1961 Kennedy representatives visited South Vietnam.
Recommended American troop intervention, but Kennedy only sent more equipment and advisers.

1962 12,000 American advisers in Vietnam (under 1,000 at Kennedy's accession).

1963 January - Communists defeated ARVN at Battle of Ap Bac.
May - Diem persecuted Buddhists.
November - unpopular Diem overthrown with encouragement of new US ambassador Lodge.

1964 August - North Vietnamese patrol boats allegedly attacked US destroyer 'Maddox' twice in the Gulf of Tonkin.
Johnson ordered first American aerial bombing of North Vietnam. Congress passed Gulf of Tonkin resolution, giving Johnson great power to wage war in Southeast Asia.
October-December - VC able to terrorise American servicemen at will in South Vietnam but Johnson (elected president 3 November) repeatedly rejected proposals for retaliation against North Vietnam.

1965 February - Johnson authorised 'Rolling Thunder' (sustained American bombing of North Vietnam).
March - First American combat troops landed in Vietnam.
June - Ky became prime minister of South Vietnam.
September - Americans beat NVA (North Vietnam's army) at Ia Drang (first big clash of conventional forces).
December - Nearly 200,000 American troops in Vietnam.

1966 Increased domestic opposition to American involvement in Vietnam.
December - nearly 400,000 US soldiers in South Vietnam.

1967 January - Hanoi offered to talk peace when US stopped bombing.
August - McNamara testified before Senate that bombing North Vietnam was ineffective.
September - Thieu elected South Vietnamese president.
December - Nearly half a million American troops in Vietnam.

1968 January - February - Tet offensive. NVA and VC attacked important South Vietnamese targets. General Westmoreland's request for more men ignored for the first time. Clark Clifford succeeded McNamara as Secretary of Defence.
March - 'Wise men' advised Johnson against further escalation. He said he would not seek re-election and wanted peace talks.
August - riots in Chicago during Democratic convention.
December - 540,000 American troops in Vietnam.

1969	March - Nixon secretly bombed Cambodia for COSVN and trail. June - First of many Nixon announcements of American troop withdrawals. October - Massive anti-war demonstrations in Washington. November - My Lai massacre made public.
1970	February - Kissinger began secret talks with North Vietnamese in Paris. April - US and ARVN forces attacked Communist sanctuaries in Cambodia - Cambodian offensive. May - Large-scale anti-war protests throughout America. December - 280,000 American troops left in Vietnam.
1971	February - Unsuccessful ARVN attack on Ho Chi Minh Trail in Laos. December - American troops down to 140,000.
1972	March - North Vietnamese offensive in South Vietnam. April - Nixon bombed Hanoi and Haiphong, confident his visits to China and USSR would leave Hanoi isolated. May - Nixon mined Haiphong harbour. August - Kissinger and Hanoi's Le Duc Tho made more and more concessions. October - Kissinger and Le Duc Tho made agreement but Thieu rejected it. Kissinger declared 'Peace is at hand.' November - Nixon re-elected. December - Nixon's 'Christmas bombing' of Hanoi and Haiphong.
1973	January - Talks resumed in Paris, finally agreed on the October terms. Cease-fire. March - Last American troops left Vietnam. April - Last American POWs released by Hanoi. August - Congress forced Nixon to stop bombing Cambodian Communists.
1974	August - Nixon resigned over Watergate scandal.
1975	April - Communists took over Cambodia and North Vietnam took over South Vietnam.
1978	Thousands of 'boat people' began fleeing Vietnam.
1982	Vietnam veterans memorial unveiled in Washington.
1990s	Slow improvement in US-Vietnamese relations culminated in Clinton's establishment of diplomatic relations.

Further Reading

Vast numbers of books about the US and Vietnam have been published. Most have been written by Americans, but many of them are available in Britain.

1 General studies

Possibly the most interesting book on the subject in general is the 700-page **Stanley Karnow**, *Vietnam: A History* (Penguin, 1991)

Karnow was an American reporter in Vietnam for many years. He covers the history of the country from the time white men first became interested in it in the seventeenth century. He naturally concentrates on the years of American involvement but is also good on the Vietnamese viewpoint. He combines a lively journalistic style with the balanced and reliably substantiated approach of the historian. There are good maps, fascinating photos, a full chronological table, biographies of principal characters, and a comprehensive index. However, the exciting narrative is relatively weak on explicit analysis and you would do well to approach the book already having obtained a good grasp of the historical debates and controversies. It is unlikely that you will have time to read the whole book, but much can be gained from a thoughtful dipping into it.

The standard American scholarly text for the war is **Robert D. Schulzinger**, *A Time for War: the United States and Vietnam, 1941-75* (Oxford University Press, 1997). Although it is heavier reading than Karnow, it is a useful work of reference.

2 Biographies

Much can be gained by seeking out the references to French Indochina and Vietnam in the following well-indexed studies of American presidents: **Stephen Ambrose**, *Eisenhower* (Simon and Schuster, 1990); **James N. Giglio**, *The Presidency of John F. Kennedy* (Kansas, 1991); **Irving Bernstein**, *Guns or Butter: the Presidency of Lyndon Johnson* (Oxford University Press, 1996); **Stephen Ambrose**, *Nixon: The Triumph of a Politician 1962-1972* and *Nixon: Ruin and Recovery 1973-1990* (Simon and Schuster, 1989 and 1991)

3 Personal memoirs

Reminiscences of American participants are plentiful and good for giving a 'feel' for Vietnam. Only a few are really well written, and even those require careful reading to elicit ideas about why America fought and failed. **Robert S. McNamara**, *In Retrospect: the Tragedy and Lessons of Vietnam* (Times Books, 1995) is a fascinating combination of admission of error and personal exoneration which does not always give the whole truth. A careful study of this book would yield plenty of ideas about the advantages and disadvantages of politicians' memoirs for you to use when answering source-based questions. From the many soldiers' memoirs **Ron Kovic**, *Born on the Fourth of July* (Corgi, 1995) is the most vivid, describing the causes, course and consequences of a young volunteer's participation in the war. One of many good photographic collections is **Tim Page**, *Nam* (Thames and Hudson, 1995). Two British TV reporters use participants' recollections to conduct a post-mortem into My Lai in **Michael Bilton and Kevin Sim**, *Four Hours in My Lai* (Penguin, 1993) which raises many issues about making moral judgements during and after wars.

4 Anthologies

A stimulating collection of writings on the causes of the war is **Jeffrey P. Kimball**, *To Reason Why: the Debate About the Causes of US Involvement in the Vietnam War* (McGraw Hill, 1990). **Walter Capps**, ed., *The Vietnam Reader* (Routledge, 1991) offers an emotional roller-coaster ride through more than 20 easy-to-read extracts from accounts of personal experiences of the war, home front and aftermath.

Index

A selection of bestselling and related titles from Hodder & Stoughton *Educational*

Title	Author	ISBN	Price (UK)
The Origins of the American Civil War: 1846-61	Alan Farmer	0 340 65868 X	£6.50
The American Civil War: 1861-65	Alan Farmer	0 340 658703	£6.50
Reconstruction and The Results of the Civil War: 1861-77	Alan Farmer	0 340 679352	£6.50
The USA and the Cold War: 1945-63	Oliver Edwards	0 340 679638	£6.50
The USA and the World: 1917-45	Peter Brett	0 340 683511	£6.50

All Hodder & Stoughton *Educational* books are available from your local bookshop, or can be ordered direct from the publisher. Just tick the titles you would like and complete the details below. Prices and availablilty are subject to change without prior notice.

Please enclose a cheque or postal order made payable to *Bookpoint Limited,* and send to: Hodder & Stoughton *Educational*, 39 Milton Park, Abingdon, Oxon OX14 4TD, UK. EMail address: orders @bookpoint.co.uk

UK postage will be charged at £2.00 for each book plus £2.30 for packing. Four books and above will be charged at 5% of the invoice value (minimum charge £5.00).

If you would like to pay by credit card, our centre team would be delighted to take your order by telephone. Our direct line (44) 01235 400414 (lines open 9.00am - 6.00pm, Monday to Saturday, with a 24 hour answering service). Alternatively you could send a fax to (44) 01235 400454.

Title _____ First name _____ Surname _____

Address _____

_____

_____

Postcode _____ Daytime telephone no. _____

If you would prefer to pay by credit card, please complete:

Please debit my Master Card / Access / Diner's Card / American Express (delete as applicable)

Card number _____

Expiry date _____ Signature _____

If you would like to receive further information on our products, please tick the box ☐